The

Sweet Potato Queens' Big~Ass Cookbook

(and Financial Planner)

Also by
Jill Conner Browne

The Sweet Potato Queens' Book of Love

God Save the Sweet Potato Queens

The
Sweet Potato Queens' Big-Ass Cookbook
(and Financial Planner)

Jill Conner
Browne

 THREE RIVERS PRESS • NEW YORK

To the most fabulous women in the world—
Vivian Neill, Cheri Anglin, Mona Shumake,
Cynthia Speetjens, Lyla Elliot, Marsha McInturff, Carol Daily,
Annie Laurie McRee, Annelle Barnett, Pippa Jackson,
Donna Sones, Sylvia Stewart, and Melanie Clement—
*the Once and Future Sweet Potato Queens, who have
dedicated themselves to living the Queenly Life and who allow
me to document it in these pages,*
To Malcolm White, *who is our Reason for Being,*
And to Kyle Jennings, *who is teaching me it's never too late
to find what you always dreamed of.*

CONTENTS

Contents

Contents

PART III

FOOD FOR BIG-ASS OCCASIONS *115*

Contents

Contents

Contents

Contents

PREFACE

Don't be misled by the title of this book. It's not your typical Betty Crocker–type cookbook, and most certainly not your Suze Orman–type financial planner. This would be on account of I ain't Betty Crocker and I sure as hell ain't Suze Orman— ask anybody.

Oh, there are recipes in here—bunches of them—and they are all quite tasty. (You can look at us and tell.) They are not what you would call your haute cuisine. Our experience with cuisine of the *haute* variety is that it's way too much trouble to do ourselves and costs way too much to have others do for us, and when they do, it looks weird. They're not happy just to plunk it on a plate and let you eat in peace; it has to be *visual*. And if it tastes good, there's only enough of it to piss us off.

We like to cook—and eat—by the vat-full. Leftovers are some of our favorite food, because then it's like somebody else cooked it—which *is* our favorite food. We dearly love Other People's Cooking. We also love Other People's Recipes, and quite a few of the recipes featured in this book were contributed by members of Sweet Potato Queen chapters, worldwide (at press time: 1,725 chapters).

The financial-planning parts of this book will no doubt be of as much value to you as they have been to us. In other words, for God's sake, get help from a qualified professional. This is a how-*not*-to book. As soon as we learn how *to,* we'll let you in on it.

Included in the Postscript, for your edification and entertainment, are the Official Rules and Regulations of the Sweet Potato Queens' Readin' and Eatin' Book Club. See our Web site (www.sweetpotatoqueens.com) for a continually unfolding panoply of news about SPQ books, events, products, and food, and for scintillating cyber-conversation.

As with the tales in my other books, everything in this one, to the best of my knowledge and recollection, is true—much to the chagrin of our Collective Mothers.

PART I

Queenly Considerations
for
Big~Ass Eatin'

1

About Betty Crocker

Merciful heavens, where do we even *start* talking about Miss B? Is it any wonder that over 50 percent of baby boomers are on Prozac? Kelly Goley, one of our favorite SPQ Wannabes (who sent us the recipe for Love Lard featured elsewhere in this book), went to Restoration Hardware (boomers love this store—it *is* our childhood) and found the same Betty Crocker cookbook that her very own mom had received for a wedding present and which little Kelly had spent many happy days in her youth poring over. (The Love Lard recipe is clearly a backlash reaction to the early-childhood trauma of being exposed to the Betty Crocker Philosophy of Feminism.)

Kelly bought the book immediately because it gave her that warm, familiar feeling of revisiting her childhood. Only when she opened the pages did she realize the havoc Mrs. Crocker had wrought on Female America, right under our noses. If you are still wondering where we as women got some of the insane ideas we have struggled with and against for the last fifty years—the addle-brained expectations that have been leveled against women from inside our ranks and out—look no further than Betty Crocker. I compared Betty's words with those of the anonymous husband who wrote *The Good Wife's Guide*, also available in the fifties. (You'll have no trouble seeing why he wouldn't put his own name on the book!)

Witness the "Helpful Hints" Mrs. Crocker offers us, while posing sweetly in a dress with an apron. She exhorts us to "perfect our homemaking skills" by practicing each task until it goes smoothly, thereby developing "techniques" for meal planning, cooking, marketing, sewing, dishwashing, home beautifying, nursing, bed-making, cleaning, and laundering. She left out yard work, auto repair and maintenance, and carpooling. Of course she did; women didn't drive much then and kids walked everywhere. And she also left out supporting the family while doing all of the above.

The Good Wife's Guide tells us that our goal is making our home a place of peace, order, and tranquillity, where our *husbands* can renew themselves in body and spirit. We should, therefore, touch up our makeup right before he comes home from work, we should not greet him with complaints or problems, we should make sure the kids are clean and quiet when he comes in. (He'll want to *look* at them but that's about all. Don't you know he's tired?) We should not complain if he's late for dinner or *even if he stays out all night*. We should count this as minor compared to what he might have gone through that day.

Well, all I have to say about that eventuality is that, unless there was an earthquake in which he was personally swallowed up and trapped for fourteen hours without food and water and with the sound of fingernails on a blackboard echoing in his ears the whole time and ants crawling all over him and he couldn't even move his hands to get them out of his nose, then he did *not* have a bad enough day to warrant him not coming home all night and me not making a peep about it, and whatever it was that *did* happen during his arduous day is nothing compared to what *will* happen when he finally does drag his sorry ass home. But that's just me. Maybe we *should* speak in a low, soothing voice and make him comfortable—possibly have him lie down in a darkened room for a spell (they have a nice one at our funeral home).

Miss Betty helpfully suggests that we develop "good work habits." This includes preparing food for tomorrow while cooking for today. Now, I do cook in vats so we can have my favorite food, leftovers, tomorrow, but Betty was suggesting that we make different dishes all at the same time or, at the very least, make different sauces to go on the same food on different days. (I can't even comment on sauces.) She also decrees that we must never run out of anything we might need in the kitchen. (We do not see her running across three neighbors' lawns with a teaspoon of vanilla and two eggs.)

Betty thought we should wear comfortable clothes (dresses— and not muumuus, either) and "properly fitted shoes" for doing housework. I get a picture of Betty and her contemporaries being "fitted" for their housework shoes. You know the shoe salesman would be vitally interested in all the housewives having comfy shoes—the better to wait on his sorry ass in. Indeed, Mr. Crocker probably personally oversaw Betty's shoe situation—for just the reason he had the oil changed in the car in a timely fashion—to save on costly repair work down the road, not to mention to prevent lost workdays should she, God forbid, get a bunion.

Betty worried about our physical needs, but not a whole lot—just offhandedly said we should eat "proper food for health and vitality." But every morning *before* our proper breakfast, we should comb our hair and put on makeup, a dash of cologne, and some simple earrings! We should alternate sitting and standing tasks so as not to be on our feet too long, but should we get tired, she recommends that we lie down on the *floor* (eyes closed) for a *full three to five minutes.* (Indeed, there she is in the book, sprawled out on the floor—dress and all.) We should always endeavor to harbor pleasant thoughts while working (there was no mention of a wood chipper in the book, so we don't know what *she* thought about) and to notice humorous and interesting incidents throughout our day so we can relate them over dinner to our shiny, clean, and smiling families.

About Betty Crocker

The Good Wife's Guide suggests that in the cooler months we might want to build a fire for Him to unwind by and that we might just imagine how catering to his comfort will provide us with immense personal satisfaction. Yes, I can just imagine it—can't you?

Betty wanted us to have a simple, appetizing cocktail (chilled in summer and warmed in winter) waiting for our weary husband when he comes home at night. And sure enough, there she is, pouring Mr. Crocker a drink from a pitcher as he sits—grinning like a mule eating briars—with his feet propped up. There is not even a glass for her in evidence—we can only hope that she drained the pitcher off-camera. And the *Good Wife* guy has one parting shot for us: *A good wife always knows her place.* I myself imagine it to be somewhere far, far away.

FINANCIAL TIP

If you have been in therapy for the last fifteen years over your failure to live up to this image of Womanhood, not to mention your inexplicable lack of desire to do so, you can save the cost of the therapist and whatever drugs you've been put on by just buying your own copy of Betty Crocker and burning it. You may stomp on it as well, before, during, and/or after the burning, but be sure to wear properly fitted footgear for this activity—your own personal do-it-yourself therapeutic exorcism.

One of the Queens—I'm sure it was Tammy—brought me a little handbook called *How to Make Love* that we might study it and further educate ourselves and others. (The Queens are dedicated to education in all areas of life, as you know.) This book was written in 1936—and it was in a series of books, all of which I wish I had on account of my thirst for knowledge. They were entitled *Fortune Telling by Cards, Facts About Nudism, Sex Facts for Men, Sex Facts for Women* (I was relieved to see they had two separate books for these—don't want anybody getting mixed up on something this important), and *84 Card Tricks*. It didn't indicate if they were listed by order of importance, but one can make certain inferences, no?

In his introduction, the author surmised that love had begun when the first man looked upon the first woman and "was satisfied with her." He indicated that this happened a very long time ago—no reference was made to her being satisfied with him, no doubt because that has not ever happened yet that anybody has heard about. At any rate, she apparently settled for him and thus Making Love began. Our author questioned how anything people had been doing for such a long time should at this late date (again, 1936) require any instructions whatsoever. However, he determined, "as in everything—man has seldom profited from his experiences of the past." Hmmm . . . I don't think there's anything we can add to that, do you?

The book explains that men were created strong and women were created weak and that, in love, the woman must always be passive. He was created chas-*er*, we were created chas-*ee*. This, the author said, accounts for our coyness at times and our illogical habits of "putting our man off." He said that we intuitively realized that in order to make ourselves more desirable, we must make ourselves less accessible. Ah, excuse me, but that sounds an awful lot like "Treat 'em like shit and never give 'em any, and they'll follow you around like a dog," does it not? It would seem that Truth is Truth, down through the ages.

He cautions us to beware mere infatuations. We should not confuse them with True Love even though they feel exactly the same in the beginning. A few questions—for us women—should help us sort things out. Can he take care of us after marriage? (No way to tell if he *will*, though.) We need to examine his faults and whether or not we can tolerate them. We may be inclined, he cautions, to say to ourselves, So what if he only bathes on Saturday night? I love him and that's all that matters. He wisely counsels us that a few *years* of breathing his stench and it will matter a lot. Do his virtues outweigh his faults? I would have to say that I can't think of any particular virtues that would weigh more in my mind than stinking to high heaven—you? Bottom line: If you think you love him and he smells like a goat, it's infatuation, not love; just go buy a goat and get happy. (The last part was my advice, not his.)

Along the lines of faults and the correcting thereof, our fellow Queen Gina wrote to us that shortly after marrying her current husband (nearly twenty years ago), she noticed his very annoying habit of not putting his dirty clothes in the hamper but choosing instead to simply pile them on the floor. Knowing as she did that no amount of nagging will have any positive effect on a man, she simply said nothing. No, she didn't *wash* his clothes, but she did put them away for him—dirty. After about two months, her mother-in-law asked her whether she knew how to launder clothes, on account of her precious boy's clothes had stains on them. Our Gina replied sweetly that yes, ma'am, she did for a fact know how to wash clothes but that he apparently didn't know squat about putting them in the hamper, and that only the clothes actually in the hamper were actually getting washed. To this very day, Mr. Gina not only puts his clothes in that hamper but he even does the laundry and helps clean the house. Makes me kind of tear up, I'm so proud. Don't you just know his mama jerked a fair-sized knot in his ass?

But back to our love guru. He instructs the guys in how to approach us for kissing purposes. It is suggested that they get us to sit on a sofa and wedge us up against the arm of it so we can't edge away. They shouldn't worry if we flinch. They shouldn't worry if we say no. They shouldn't worry if we flinch, say no, and try to get up. They should hold us in place and reassure us and continue on with their plan unless we flinch, say no real loud, try to get up, and commence scratching their eyes out—then, and only then, should they back off and try to get *themselves* out of a "bad situation." He attributes our reluctance to accept their advances to the fact that we probably still believe that we can get pregnant from kissing. It couldn't possibly be that we would rather kiss our dog's butt.

When it comes to marriage, we are all instructed to marry

the healthy. He says that an ailing woman is a menace to any love affair (he clearly had never been nurse to a sick man)—the woman needs to be strong enough to do housework, to bear children, and to help *build the house.* I think I threw the book across the room about then.

Queen Wendy from West Virginia wrote to sing the praises of her husband, who thoughtfully takes one of the dogs and goes off hunting for a couple of months every year while she stays behind with the house dog, lolling by the fire that he carefully constructed before his departure, drinking beer, eating sweet, salty, fried, and au gratin stuff, and generally Not Doing Jack Shit. She says that husband of hers is cute as a button, was raised by a good mama, and denies Queen Wendy nothing—and no, he ain't for hire. But Wendy has remembered all her life a baby-sitter she had when she was eight years old—Judy. Judy was married to a man who needed killing, but fortunately some other woman lured him away from her before she actually did it.

Wendy remembers, "After the dickhead moved out, he called Judy and asked that she bring him his truck and his clothes. He actually said, 'Oh, and by the way, wash my truck for me before you drop it off.' Judy—nice wife that she was—promptly gathered up his clothes, hangers and all, and carefully put them (in wads) in the back of his pickup. She then loaded all of us kids in the truck with her and we went to the drive-through car wash. Judy has always been a role model for me." As she is for us all.

FINANCIAL TIP

See how smart it was of Judy to combine her tasks like that? Washing the clothes and the truck at the same time saved both time and money. We can all learn from her example.

Queen Tracey tells us she desperately wants a "Men Are All Idiots and I Am Married to Their King" T-shirt. It's admittedly one of our favorites, but I don't know where to get another one these days. Maybe me and Tammy will make some for the Web site; it does seem to be a popular theme. The very evening that Queen Tracey was to go to her book club to discuss *The Sweet Potato Queens' Book of Love,* her husband—who is a mechanic and therefore qualifies as a Man Who Can Fix Things—managed to drop an *entire* car on his foot. So instead of going to the meeting, she had to drive his ass to the emergency room. "I can tell you I wasn't happy with my five-year-old son. He was responsible for releasing the jack, thus allowing the car to fall on my husband's foot in the first place. If I have told that boy once, I have told him a thousand times, wait until Daddy is *completely* under the car before releasing the jack!" Her zippity-do-dah vision (of her outfit at his funeral) was brief at best—turned out it didn't even break his foot. If you think about it though, this was much better for Tracey. If you can't kill 'em, for God's sake, don't maim 'em unless they don't live with you anymore. Who you think's gonna have to wait on 'em when they're laid up?

About Betty Crocker

Tracey has a friend, named Tammy, as it turns out, who also needs a "Men Are All Idiots" shirt. It seems that Tammy's husband had a pesky habit of keeping his fish bait in the refrigerator with the family food supplies. Despite repeated pleas from Tammy regarding the carton full of maggots, said carton remained ensconced in the fridge; it wasn't on the husband's calendar to go fishing in the immediate future and he wanted the bait to remain "fresh." *As if.* Tammy threw up her hands and knew there wasn't but One Thing Left to Do—yep, it was time to stir-fry. Oh yeah, baby, Tammy stir-fried the sumbitch's own maggots and fed 'em to him. According to Tracey and Tammy, "It was a scene right out of Barbie's Dream House!" And the really good part is, a few days later, when he was bitching about his missing maggots, she could, with a completely straight face and in utter truthfulness, swear on a stack of Bibles that she did *not* throw them out.

FINANCIAL TIP

I don't include a stir-fry recipe for maggots or any other fish bait, but I'm sure any good recipe you already have would work—just wherever it talks about shrimp or chicken, substitute maggots. But hey—talk about your money-saver! I don't know for certain, but I'd be willing to bet that maggots are a whole lot cheaper than chicken breasts.

Lest my dear readers be left with that taste in your mouth, omigod, do I have a treat for you—a secret too good to keep.

Right in our very midst, in the Worldwide SPQ Movement, we have a bona fide Betty Crocker Award winner and a deliciously appropriate recipe to go with it. Mary Anne Tomlinson of Nashville's own Music City Queens is our girl, but don't think this fact was easily acquired. Here's the story behind it:

Mary Anne, it seems, in the course of a convoluted conversation with her good pal Mary, revealed that she had a friend named Nancy who had been the rightful and just recipient of the (Jackson, Mississippi) Murrah High School Typing Award. Keep in mind, Nancy won this back when it really meant something, when typewriters were manual—not even a correction key—made of solid iron, and weighed about seventy-five hundred pounds each. Friend Mary was most impressed. And so it was that Mary Anne then felt herself goaded into bragging that Nancy was not the *only* one who had been a prizewinner back in high school. Why she, Mary Anne herself, had won the home economics award, or as Mary Anne calls it, the "Betty-by-God-Crocker Award," for two years running!

And we all know what that means. Betty-by-God-Crocker was, after all, Betty-by-God-Crocker long before Martha Stewart ever thought about walking on custom-dyed water.

So it seems only natural that a few years back, around Christmastime, Mary Anne and her daughter, Carrie, were spending a lovely afternoon at home preparing to make divinity. Mary Anne was waxing motherly and dispensing all manner of invaluable divinity-making advice—about how the forces of Mother Nature all have to work in your favor and you must do various and sundry things to please the Divinity Gods or you will be forced to eat your divinity with a spoon. (In all fairness, I would be compelled to tell Carrie, as I would my own precious Bailey, that if being forced to eat one's divinity with a spoon numbers among the Worst Things That Ever Happen to You— and may it, please God, be so—then we should all be Eternally and Abundantly Grateful. It's way better than glaucoma, as Dan Jenkins taught us.)

No~Spoons~Necessary Divinity

At any rate, Mary Anne told Carrie that one must (STEP 1) wait for a day on which the following criteria are met: It must be cold, it must be sunshiney, and there must be *absolutely no chance* of rain. These conditions having been met, one must then (STEP 2) don a lacy apron and a strand of pearls before even crossing the threshold of the kitchen. As she was relating all this Betty-by-God-Crocker–type wisdom to her baby girl, Mary Anne suddenly thought of a totem more powerful than pearls that she could put on for the cooking process, one that would surely impress and appease whatever Divinity Gods there may be: She would wear her actual Betty-by-God-Crocker medals. And so it was that the actual making of the divinity got put on hold for quite some time while Mary Anne went to the attic to do a headfirst thing into her old trunk full of high-school crap until she produced, for Carrie's edification and wonder, the Medals Themselves. We imagine that Carrie had not fully grasped the reality of just exactly Who Her Mother Was until that time—it had to have been a defining moment in their relationship. (Mary Anne included in her letter to me photos of what *appear* to be two Betty-by-God-Crocker medals. We trust and believe that they are two separate and distinct medals and not merely two photographs of the *same* medal. I do admit to being impressed.)

Before finally giving us the recipe, Mary Anne further cautions that, besides the apron and the pearls (and the Betty-by-God-Crocker medals if you have them, but we're sure the Divinity Gods know just how hard they are to come by and won't hold it against those of us who don't have them), you will also need a helper and a candy thermometer.

And so we begin to make divinity by (STEP 3) stirring together 2½ cups sugar, ½ cup light Karo, ½ cup water, and ¼ teaspoon salt. Then (STEP 4) cook that, stirring all the while, over medium heat until the sugar dissolves and it reaches 260 degrees or "hard-ball" stage. You'd best be stirring it all the time and you'd best (STEP 5) have that candy thermometer handy. As soon as the thermometer registers the desired temp, (STEP 6) remove the Karo stuff from the heat immediately.

Unless you have extra appendages that we don't know about, get that helper of yours to (STEP 7) start beating **2 egg whites** back when you are heating up the sugar stuff. Okay, then you will need to (STEP 8) gradually pour a thin stream of the syrup mixture over the egg-white peaks while your helper is still beating the stew out of the stuff with the mixer. When the Karo drizzling is finished, (STEP 9) add in **1 teaspoon vanilla** while one of you (STEP 10) beats the concoction on high speed for another 5 minutes. When you can pick up your beaters and get stiff peaks, you are ready to (STEP

11) drop the stuff by teaspoonfuls onto wax paper and (STEP 12) stick a pecan half on top of each one and give it a little push. And now, *oh man,* you've got *divinity!*

If you have done absolutely everything right and it is your lucky day, it will harden in just a few minutes—until it melts in your mouth. Some people add a little red or green food coloring to their divinity—but we don't associate with them. Divinity is white and there's really nothing we can do about that.

2

Pass the Salt, Please!

Of all the things we love to eat—and Lord knows that's nearly 'bout everything but anchovies—our words would not rank in the top three. Don't you just hate it when you make some big pronouncement—or worse, a judgment about somebody else's behavior—and then, bigger'n Dallas, the very next thing you know, there *you* are, doing that very thing? And do not think for one minute that nobody will notice or remember your big talk. They notice and they are gleeful—which is only right. We would do—and have done—the same for them on many occasions after all.

So what I'm getting around to here is some words that I my ownself have been forced—albeit happily so—to devour. These would be the words I wrote in my first book, *The Sweet Potato Queens' Book of Love*, saying with no small degree of vehemence that we don't want anything to do with any guy who's younger than we are. I go on at great length about this and cite examples of people I have personally known who dared, in my presence, to date the Young. I am not kind.

Funny thing I've noticed as I've gotten older—which I do a little bit of every day without exception: Every single, solitary thing I have ever looked down my pug nose at or berated somebody else for doing or that I've been shocked, appalled, and dismayed at the very thought of—I have lived to do that very thing my very ownself. "Chagrin" seems apropos, and I am chagrined. It's the least I can do. Of late, whenever I catch myself saying, "I would *never* do" whatever, I gasp in horror and try to quickly take it back or change my words in a futile attempt to trick karma. But it never works. Once I have uttered the fatal "N" word, I am doomed to perform, in spades, the very thing I said "never" to. Sigh.

And so we come back to where I started with this whole rant—the Younger Man issue. After all the derision I've heaped on countless others for their fascination with the Young, what else could the gods decree but that I be totally smitten, knocked sideways, and slapped silly by a hunka-hunka burnin' *young* love—the Cutest Boy in the World.

I'll tell you how it happened. (Now, *he* has an entirely different version he likes to tell, but he ain't the one writin' this book, so I'm telling it my way, which has the added advantage of being the truth.) I was in Mobile, Alabama, to participate in a book and author event, and there he was: the Cutest Boy in the World. He had published a book for one of the other authors. After the event, we chatted briefly and congenially and I left for the Page and Palette bookstore in nearby Fairhope, Alabama—which, as it happened, was right across the street from the office of the Cutest Boy in the World.

After my book signing, it seemed only neighborly to stroll over to see him and his partner, the ineffable Sonny Brewer, and so I did. During the course of my visit, the Cutest Boy in the World suggested, in an offhand manner, that we might have a drink or something together that evening. I commented that, although I would purely *love* to do that very thing, regrettably I had yet another book signing in a nearby town and had to drive home to Jackson that night. I left hoping that I might hear from him in the next few weeks or so. Sadly, I did not. (Now, *he* likes to tell it that he asked me out and I gave him a withering glance and said *no* and left him with no hope whatsoever that in this lifetime I would even consider going out with him. Let me just say this about that: Nobody who's ever *seen* him believes it for a second. I mean, he is, after all, the Cutest Boy in the World. It's just not possible that I turned him down. The good thing, as it turned out later, was that he *thought* I had turned him down which, predictably and thankfully, only served to make him want me so much more.)

Pass the Salt, Please!

So about a year passed, during which I never heard from him. Then, in late March 2001, I found myself headed back to Fairhope for a book signing for *God Save the Sweet Potato Queens*, and one of the Queens, Tammy, was going with me. We pulled up in front of the store, and no sooner had the car come to a complete stop than I looked out the side window, and who did I see, peering in at me, but the Cutest Boy in the World! Color *me* happy!

He toted all our stuff to the bookstore and generally made us comfy, fetching stuff and whatnot during the signing. Not willing to let him get away from me again, I asked *him* to have a drink with us after we finished, and he accepted. During our conversation over drinks, Tammy and I suggested that he meet us the next day at the Pensacola Barnes & Noble and then go with us to the Florabama—it's on the Florida/Alabama line—the best beach bar in the world.

As we parted company that evening, he gave us directions for a "shortcut" (a euphemism, as we all know, for "Go this way and never be seen nor heard from again in this life") to a restaurant we wanted to try on our way down to the beach. We set off on the road he specified and had gone no more than thirty feet when Tammy, who was driving, saw in the rearview mirror her own reflection, which was bluish around the edges. Yep, flashing blue lights were looming large atop a cop car that was apparently in hot pursuit of us. Sighing, Tammy pulled over and let her window down so her charm could fly undiluted directly into the face of the policeman. He never had a chance.

He appeared to be about twelve, and when he took Tammy's license to call and see if she was a wanted felon or not, I said, "Ask him if his mama knows he's out here in that car." (When did cops start being twelve? I guess about the same time we started being a hundred, huh?) Anyway, he knew how to operate the radio, and there were no outstanding warrants for Tammy at that particular time, so he let us off with a very stern, trying-to-sound-grown-up warning.

Tammy flashed her pearly whites and gave him, I swear to God, one of my "business" cards—they're hot pink and say, LICK YOU ALL OVER 10 CENTS—ASK ABOUT OUR OTHER SPECIALTIES! And he just grinned and she grinned right back, and I leaned over and said, "Now, honey, you be real particular how you use that card, you hear?" He grinned some more, and we whizzed on off into the night, down the road specified by the Cutest Boy in the World.

We rode and we rode and we rode and we never got anywhere that looked like anyplace we wanted to be, and Tammy snatched up the cell phone and flung it at me. "Call that boy!" she shrieked, and so I did. As soon as he answered, I just said, "We are lost as shit out here and it is your fault and therefore it is your job to get your ass out here and find us and feed us. We are tired and lost and hungry." My whine reached a pitch so high bats couldn't have heard it, and all I could hear on the other end was the Cutest Boy in the World *laughing*. He had realized as soon as we drove off, he said, that he'd given us the wrong directions, and he was just waiting to hear from us. Where are you now, he wanted to know, and we just screeched back at him that if we knew that, we wouldn't be calling his sorry ass. This point-less exchange went on for some little while until Tammy finally identified a landmark to pinpoint our mysterious location and he told her how to get on track. We eventually did get to the restaurant, where we ordered every item on the menu that contained cheese in any amount.

After all this, he wasn't at the signing the next day, and we were fairly distraught. Tammy hit me in the head with the cell phone until I agreed to call him. Our conversation went something like this: "Where the hell *are* you?" "Where the hell are *you?*" "We're almost to the Florabama. Git your ass down here!" "I'll be there in a half hour." And he was. After many hours of dancing and talking, he got around to kissing me and that was, as they say, *it.* I was ass over teacups in love with him at that very moment.

It wasn't long before I determined that we had a little age-disparity thing going on, and it gave me pause. Only a pause. It amounted to a clutch—not brakes—and I went right on falling in love with him, even though I couldn't quite tune out the echo of my own words of condemnation.

The Cutest Boy in the World is almost exactly ten years younger than I am, and I do love him something awful, but damn, I wish he was old or fat or homely or something—instead of, well, perfect. He is sweet and smart and funny and bright and talented and strong and generous and honest and loving and kind and decent and cheerful and optimistic and compassionate and sensitive and honorable and understanding *and* he's built like a brick shithouse. I mean, if there's a flaw in this guy, I haven't found it yet and, Lord knows, I've been looking at him pretty close. Excuse me, did I mention that he can also Fix Things? Anything, anything at all, he can fix it.

But early on in our relationship, the age issue reared its head. I mentioned in passing that probably my favorite song in the whole world is "Soothe Me" by Sam and Dave, and with a completely straight face, the man said to me, "Who's Sam and Dave?" And I'm like—*Whu-u-u-ut?* Sam and Dave are like *Sam and Dave,* man! You know, Sam and Dave. Blank—he's totally blank—no earthly idea who I'm talking about. (If you're under forty, you probably share his confusion.) So, in that split second, I'm thinking to myself, How is it possible that I am embarking on an intimate relationship with a man who *totally missed Motown* because he wasn't born yet? An excellent question and one that haunted me until I posed it for my dear friend Malcolm White (yes, *that* Malcolm—the one who founded the St. Paddy's Parade in our hometown).

Malcolm, I said, you've had some experience Dating the Young. Speak to me about a situation that's gnawin' at me. How, I asked, can I even think about getting serious about a Man Who Totally Missed Motown? And Malcolm, in the vast wisdom he's amassed in his abundant experience on this earth, said to me, Well, yeah, that's *one* way to look at it. But think about it this way, he counseled: You get to be there *with* somebody the very first time they hear Motown. Can you even remember hearing Motown for the very first time? And we got all off into the miracle of Motown and wishing we could unhear it so we could start all over with it again. Sort of like re-virgination, I suppose.

So, anyway, Malcolm helped me get over the Young issue. But another occasion finally sealed the deal. In the last chapter of *God Save the Sweet Potato Queens*, I wrote about how the Only Man I Ever Really Loved, Winston Brown, had upped and died and about how our song had been "Workin' in a Coal Mine." Now, what I didn't say is that when I stood by his open casket and kissed him for the last time on this earth, I said to him, "Winston, you have got to help me find love. You are the only one I ever believed really loved me. How will I ever find love again? Help me find it!" All the while I was sobbing and my tears were getting him sopping wet. It was sincere, but it wasn't very pretty. (I do have a point here and I'm getting to it, I swear.)

Move ahead from the casket scene a couple of years and see me chancing upon the Cutest Boy in the World, who seems perfect in every way except I'm afraid he's too young. See the quandary I am wallowing in over the whole thing. A few weeks later, see me and the Queens at a big party put on for us by Susan Daigre at Bookends in Bay St. Louis, Mississippi (just about the best little bookstore in the best little beach town in the world), and see the Cutest Boy in the World joining us there. See us all dancing with wild abandon to a band by the name of Benny Grunch and the Bunch. Okay, you've got the picture, we're all there just having a big time when the band announces they'll play one more song before they take a break, and what do you reckon they broke into? "Workin' in a Coal Mine"! Now,

I ask you, what are the odds? When in your life have you ever been anywhere that the band played "Workin' in a Coal Mine"? It's not exactly Top 40. It took me so by surprise, I immediately burst into tears and scurried off into another room, and one of the Queens—I'm sure it was Tammy because she knew that was my and Winston's song—was just beaming at me. "It is a sign," she said, "Winston's giving you a sign. This is your gift from the Universe. Get back out there!" And the cloud just lifted off my life, and I've been in lo-o-o-o-ove ever since.

I suggested that we both be forty-four, which is neither my age nor his but is somewhere in the middle, and he went for it! What a guy—did I tell you or what? The Tammys and I were talking about it and we decided that forty-four is the perfect age: It's enough over forty to have some sense and enough under fifty not to really be terrified of it yet. So forty-four we are, and forty-four we shall remain. Feel free to join us, whatever age you happen to be.

FINANCIAL TIP

Okay, granted, there's a lot to be said for rich old guys with bad hearts and no relatives, but you can't always get what you want. This cannot be news to you. So look on the bright side. The young guy will be able to work much harder for many more years in order to support you, and he's likely to be healthy enough to take care of you in the years prior to the nursing home. And think of the money you'll save on Viagra: By the time he needs it, you'll be dead.

Trouble Monkey

Now, what recipe shall we have here . . . something that goes down easy when one is Eating One's Own Words. Oh my, we're going to need alcohol to wash those pesky words down, aren't we? This is something called a Trouble Monkey, invented by the Cutest Boy in the World for Bruce Browning and Tammy. You want **3 parts Absolut Mandarin, 2 parts Ocean Spray cranberry juice, 1 part Seven-Up,** and the **juice of** $^1/_2$ **orange.** Squeeze juice into drink and then put the mashed-up orange in it, too.

One of the many benefits of my altogether felicitous relationship with the Cutest Boy in the World—or I guess it would be more accurate to say two of the many benefits—are the mom and dad of the Cutest Boy in the World, Bill and Billie Sue Jennings, or simply Mom and Dad. If two sweeter people have ever drawn breath, well, trot 'em out here—I'll just have to see for myself. I am convinced that these *are* the two sweetest people who've ever drawn breath, but that's not all—oh, no, there's so-o-o much more. For instance, Dad can wiggle his ears. I'm not talking about just sliding his scalp back and forth and creating the appearance of movement in the ear area. I'm telling you the man can flap his ears like Dumbo and he can do them one at a time. Plus, he can slick 'em back to his head—he calls that his "racing form." Doubtless it's not the only reason Mom's been married to him for coming up on fifty years—but you gotta believe it's been a contributing factor.

Sweet Potato (Queen) Cornbread

Mom's is the ultimate example of a life well-lived. I am in total awe of her. She's smart, accomplished, beautiful—inside and out—loving, courageous, and bubbling over with the sheer joy of living. It's been an easy fifty years for Dad, clearly. To further endear her to me personally, she and her friends turn out some excellent eats! Mom herself makes this sweet potato cornbread that is worth driving all the way to Mountain Pine, Arkansas, for, but you won't have to—here's how to do it. Mix together this dry stuff: **1 cup all-purpose flour, 1 cup yellow cornmeal, 4 teaspoons baking powder, 1 teaspoon salt,** and **½ cup sugar.** Separately, mix together this wet stuff: **3 sweet potatoes,** cooked and mashed (or you *may* use **1 16-ounce can of sweet potatoes,** and in this recipe, it really is okay not to use home-cooked ones, I would tell you if it mattered), **2 eggs, 6 tablespoons milk,** and **3 tablespoons oil.** Then mix the dry stuff and the wet stuff, just until it's all moist (don't beat it to death), then put it in greased muffin tins and bake at 425 until done—usually about 15 to 20 minutes.

Linda's Perky Pickles

Mom's friends have also contributed to my eating pleasure during my frequent visits. Linda Brod makes sure there are two giant jars of these pickles waiting for me—we eat one while I'm there and I get to take one home. What a deal! I cannot stop eating these things if they're in front of me, and I'm not a big pickle person as a rule. To make Linda's Perky Pickles, just buy a **gallon of regular ole dill pickles**—the great big whole ones—and bring 'em home and drain 'em, reserving the juice. Slice up the big pickles into handier munching size and put 'em in some quart jars. Then take all that pickle juice and measure it out so you have **1 cup pickle juice** per quart jar, but don't put it in the jars yet—put it in a pan and add to it **1¹/₃ cup sugar** per quart jar and heat it just until the sugar is dissolved. Then you can either go on and pour it into the pickle jars, cap 'em, and put 'em in the refrigerator, or you can do what I do and add some juice from a jar of jalapeño peppers to it. I just add the pepper juice a little bit at a time and keep tasting it until it's the right amount of sweet and hot to suit me—I suggest the same method to you. But I like 'em either way, with the hot stuff or without. I expect you will as well.

Linda's Killer Cake with No Apples

Linda also makes this killer cake that makes me think of apple cake—but there's no apple in it, so go figger. You just take a **regular ole yellow cake mix** and make it with **4 eggs, ³/₄ cup oil,** and **one cup water,** but before you put it in the pan to bake it, stir in **1 can Betty Crocker Rich and Creamy Coconut Pecan Frosting**— that's right, you put it *in* the cake and then you just bake it at 350 for about an hour or until it's beautiful and you can't stand it anymore.

Actual Apple Cake

If the yen for a cake that tastes like apples is so strong that you don't even mind going to some trouble for it, Mom offers this Actual Apple Cake. The biggest pain in the construction of this cake is the peeling of the apples, but in the grand scheme of things, it's not really what you'd call an overwhelming task, so go for it. You want about **3 cups of apples,** peeled and chopped, for this cake—do this part first and the rest is easy, easy. Mix together **1⅓ cups canola oil, 2 cups sugar,** and **2 large eggs,** and beat it till it's creamy. Sift together **2½ cups flour, 1 teaspoon baking soda, 1 teaspoon salt,** and **1 teaspoon baking powder,** and gradually add the dry mix to the creamy mix until you have one mix that's thoroughly mixed, then put in **1 running-over teaspoon vanilla** and mix that in. Now gently mix in your apples and **1 cup chopped pecans.** Put it in a greased 9-by-13-inch pan and bake it at 350 for close to an hour (don't wander off and burn the thing after you went to the trouble of making an actual apple cake from scratch). I like to let it cool off just enough that you can get a big hunk of it out of the pan without it just falling apart (although it tastes every bit as good fallen apart) and put a big glob of actual whipped cream on top of it and just lap it all up and then maybe take a nap.

That Pumpkin Stuff That Dorothy Makes

Mom's friend Dorothy Frazier makes this pumpkin stuff that will make you the most popular one at any potluck dinner you ever attend. (I know, just the thought of pumpkin goobs some people out, but trust me, folks will gnaw off their neighbor's arm to get at this stuff.) I'm sure it has a real name, but we just call it That Pumpkin Stuff That Dorothy Makes. You mix together **1 16-ounce can of pumpkin** and a **can of Pet evaporated milk,** and then you add **1 cup sugar,** ½ **teaspoon cinnamon,** ½ **teaspoon nutmeg,** and **3 eggs.** Then you put that stuff in a greased 9-by-13-inch pan and crumble **1 yellow (butter) cake mix** (we use Duncan Hines) and **1 cup chopped pecans** on top of it and then you pour **2 sticks melted butter** over it. (It's hard even to write that with a straight face—*two sticks?* Yes, ma'am—yum, no?) Bake it for 50 to 60 minutes at 350.

While you let it cool off, make the frosting by mixing together **8 ounces cream cheese, 1 cup powdered sugar,** and **2 cups Cool Whip,** then smear it on top of the pumpkin stuff and put some more pecans on top. Then force yourself to put it in the refrigerator until it's time to go to the potluck dinner; otherwise you won't have any left to take. When you get there, immediately serve yourself a big wad of it and go off somewhere safe to eat it, because once the next person tastes it, it's over—they'll be swarming over it like yellow jackets on a KFC bag.

If all these goodies—and the Cutest Boy in the World—aren't worth eating a few words, nothing is!

3

Getting Old

Getting Old is positively *stunning*, in the true sense of the word—as in being knocked sideways by a gun of the stun variety. You look in the mirror every day of your life for years, taking for granted that when you do so, you will see yourself, and you do; so you feel pretty secure about the process. And then one day, with no warning whatsoever, you look in that same mirror, expecting to see that same face, and what do you find? You find this *old* person looking back at you with a baleful stare. Upon closer inspection, you discover it to be *you*—in an old-lady suit, which has apparently permanently affixed itself to your person.

Getting Old

You've got old-lady hair. It's going gray and the texture of it is no longer hairlike but more like string or perhaps straw that the cat has seen fit to suck on all day. Your skin has turned against you somehow; indeed, it seems it would crawl completely off your frame if possible. It *feels* like snakeskin actually. If only it might split open and allow you to crawl off in a shiny, new skin, leaving the old dried-up husk to crisp in the sun. But no, in it you must remain.

You gaze in horror at some formerly familiar body part—your arm, for instance—and notice with a shudder that when you bend it as you have done a million times a day for your entire life with no ill effect, the skin ripples and wrinkles in a bizarre fashion. Whose arm is that hanging from your body? you ask. And have you looked at your knees lately? Don't even bother. Just trust me—it's bad.

Moles have started to reproduce themselves at will all over your body but show a particular fondness for your chest, neck, and back. One might be considered a "beauty mark"; one *thousand* and you've moved past overkill—it's distracting, at best. And, we note happily, moles now come in many shapes, sizes, and colors. I'd have to say the skin-tag types are my favorites—right up there with the ones that overnight grow a six- to seven-inch *hair* smack in the middle of 'em.

And, of course, your eyesight is so bad you might easily go several entire days before you realize you have got this long—usually black—hair sticking straight out of the side of your face. You normally don't see it yourself; someone else—a small, very loud child in the checkout line or your ex-husband's new child-bride or possibly, the worst-case scenario, your very own *boyfriend*—will notice it and give it a little tug.

One of the reasons your eyesight is so poor is that your upper eyelids are spending most of their time hanging down into your actual line of sight instead of perching up there above your eyes displaying eye shadow, the way nature intended.

There seem to be two choices (or rather destinies—for who would actively *choose* either one?): You turn out to be one of those stringy, beef-jerky-looking old ladies or you're fat.

Let me address the Under Forty readers here for just a moment. First of all, you should know that, in my opinion, you are larva. It's a wonder you even have all your hands and feet. You really can't fathom this right now—I know because I remember—but you are a *baby* and you should not be out loose running around unsupervised. Trust me, nearly every choice you're making today is the wrong one, but take heart. Crazy as it sounds, it's apparently what you are supposed to be doing—*nobody* does it any different. And the consequences of all the stupid crap you are doing today, which you will regret, will make you a Fabulous Woman in just a few short years!

Go look in the mirror right this second. I know, you think you're a mess. But hey, *listen to me!* If you are under forty, you are a precious, darling *girl*, and you should put on the skimpiest garment you can legally wear in public and commence prancing around in it night and day because I promise that in about ten years, you are going to look back at photographs of yourself and say, "My God—I was *perfect!* What was I thinking? If I looked like that today, I would rule the world!" Tammy and I were talking about it just the other day. If we had had any sense of how very cute we were back then, we would have run naked down the middle of the street. Honeychile, you ain't never gonna look this good again in your life, and you'd better be making that hay while the sun is shining 'cause I am here to tell you that a change is gonna come!

Now, while you're appreciating your current cuteness, run out and have your picture taken—the one you will want used in your obituary, especially if you plan on living a whole lot longer. We see it all the time in the paper here: an obit with a picture of a winsome lass with a fetching smile and a devilish twinkle in her eye—a sweet young thing. When you read the obit to find out how someone so young was snatched from this earth in such an untimely fashion, you learn that she was actually ninety-seven years old when she died. Trust me, you could drag your picture behind your car and leave it out in the rain and sun for two years, and it would fare better than *you* will in the aging process. Getting old is the rudest awakening you will ever have: It is the ultimate slap in the face with a wet squirrel.

You are probably anticipating aging with some degree of humor—and denial. Oh, I know all about that. My best bud, Rhonda Abel, and I used to plan—when we were fourteen—how we would dye our hair blue. We would wear cinnamon-colored hose with reinforced heels and toes and roll them down at the knees. We would wear polyester short-sleeved, round-necked dresses that we had made ourselves. Mine was to be "a lovely shade of turquoise with patch pockets of royal blue" (all this is from an actual note we exchanged in the eighth grade, which I still have). Our shoes would be those stretchy gold metallic things with the toes that curl up, which come in a bag in the sock department. We would take up smoking and keep one cigarette burning in an ashtray and one hanging off our lower lip at all times, especially while we're talking, so it would kind of flop up and down and sling ashes all over. We would have deep, raspy, whiskey-sounding voices and we would yell a lot and be real crabby all the time and scream at the neighborhood kids to get out of our yards. We would have our hair ratted up professionally once a week and never comb it otherwise, and wrap our heads in toilet paper and put on big hair nets at night. We would wear glasses—thick, ugly ones—whether we needed them or not, with silver chains attached to keep them hanging around our necks when not in use. Our homes would be filled with ugly ceramic souvenirs and brightly painted statues of children with big eyes and small dogs. We would find useless items made from two-liter Coke bottles, coat hangers, and yarn to be wildly irresistible, and we would cover all our furniture with clear plastic to "save" it.

We planned to do all of this when we turned the ripe old age of forty—knowing, as we did with the infinite wisdom that is the exclusive domain of the incredibly young, that life would be completely over by then, anyway, so why not? My fortieth birthday was ten years ago and I don't feel any different from the way I did at fourteen when I wrote that note to Rhonda. That's what's so maddening about getting old: You still *feel* young and cute!

FINANCIAL TIP

You know all those songs that exhort you to "shake your money-maker"? Listen to 'em and shake while the shakin' is good because your entire body will turn into a veritable money pit before you can say "bilateral blepharoplasty" or even "eye job," for that matter. My advice to you is to go out and buy the cheapest clothes and makeup available on the open market; it doesn't matter, you'll look fabulous in them. Take the money you save and put it in something interest-bearing. Consider it a trust fund for your old self, because trust me, it costs the proverbial shitload of money to maintain an old woman.

Just go on and decide you're gonna have blond hair one day—no matter what color your hair is today. The technology does not exist in the world today to enable any hair colorist to replicate "brunette." If you have brown hair as a sweet young thing and you try to carry that color with you into your old age, you will either have red hair or green hair. Cosmetics. Oh, Lord. Pre-forty, you can wash your face with Tide and use Vaseline for moisturizer, toss on a little mascara and lip gloss, and you're a friggin' cover girl. Those of us on the slippery slope that is the Other Side of Forty can testify—those days are *so over*. You will pore over labels promising everything short of actual rebirth—you will buy most of them for an average of $450 per quarter ounce—and none of them will work. You will still be getting older and poorer with every passing purchase.

Your clothes will be much larger—*more* fabric costs *more* money—and they will have to be engineered much better than the clothes of your youth. Getting your tits off your waist and your butt off the back of your knees requires not just clothing but architecture, sweetie.

You will wake up one day with a man (who himself has put on at least twenty-five pounds since you've known him) telling you, with a straight face, that, in his considered opinion, your recent lack of resiliency is probably due to *your* weight gain. We heard from a woman to whom a man had mentioned that her butt was a little too much on the big side. (How he could even see her butt over his own gut hanging to his knees is a still-unsolved mystery.) And he shared this tidbit with her while they were having sex! Properly horrified on her behalf, we asked her what she did about it. She replied that she exercised her best option: She never had sex with him again! Since she had resolved on the spot that he would never see *her* naked again, sex became problematic anyway, and she divorced him a few months later. I sincerely hope she never cooked for him again, either.

Your hormones have caused you nothing but heartache and tears, pain and money since you were thirteen. Guess what? It's not over. If you've lived with a teenager lately, you will know what's in store for you shortly. Apparently it doesn't matter if the hormones are flowing or ebbing; insanity ensues either way—and in my observation, there's not a lot of difference in the behaviors. Menopausal women are pretty much like teenagers—crazy as loons.

FINANCIAL TIP

Menopause is yet another reason to start that trust fund for yourself while you're young. Being crazy costs a lot. You have to go see a lot of different medical professionals about yourself and pay for a number of different medications to try to control yourself. Menopausal women also pay exorbitant utility bills in the summertime; the air conditioner has not yet been made that can cope with a hot flash. You have to keep yourself in cold storage all the time, just in case. You can always get naked when a hot flash strikes (and you will, regardless of where you are), but the room must be pre-chilled or it doesn't help. For those of you living in a cold climate, there would be some semi-good news in that you won't have to run the heat in the wintertime. Unfortunately, for those of us in the Deep South, however, well, we have to run the a/c practically year round.

Hormones are some serious juju, and if you don't get them sorted out, you might find that you also need money for things like lawyers and bail even. A couple of the Queens—Tammy and Tammy—and I went on Delbert McClinton's Sandy Beaches Cruise, or as we call it, the Delbert Cruise or the Blues Cruise (www.delbert.com—sign up and go; you cannot imagine just how fine it truly is). And we met a delightful little woman whose boyfriend had broken up with her the week before the cruise. Now, our first question was, naturally, How stupid is *he?* It was a purely rhetorical question since we already had a pretty good idea of the answer. Anyway, she posted hilarious stuff on her cabin door, and there was usually a traffic jam of women reading her door and laughing hysterically. She had a picture of this perfectly gorgeous guy in a Speedo with the caption "No matter how perfectly gorgeous he is, some woman somewhere is SICK OF HIS SHIT." And isn't that just the truth?

She also posted an actual news clipping from Toronto, with the headline WOMAN YANKS OFF BOYFRIEND'S TESTICLES. Now, you would hardly need to read any further to be howling with glee, but we read it all and it was worth it. The article went into great detail about how this couple had gotten into a helluva fight and somehow, in the course of things, the woman managed to literally snatch the balls right off the guy's body. From where I'm sitting, that is some heavy-duty snatchin'. She was in jail (they didn't describe her mood, but we imagine it was pretty peaceful—I mean, after all, that's one guy who won't be doing *her* wrong again), and he was in surgery, where they were attempting to reattach the snatched spheres.

His doctor didn't hold out much hope, however, for the success of the operation. The doctor had been interviewed, and he was supposed to be talking doctorly and all, but what he said was that you could do this and that and the other thing (medical-sounding jargon), but "generally, in a case like this, it's good-bye, Charlie." Excuse me, *good-bye, Charlie* is a medical prognosis? The guy's doctor is having his day in the sun with the press at the expense of his patient's personal testicles, and with the weight of umpteen years of medical school and experience behind him, he says, *"Good-bye, Charlie"*? We were screaming. The precious woman came out and told us that the man staying in the cabin next to hers was decidedly nervous and kept to himself a lot.

The thing about this story is that (besides being hilarious) it supports our recommendation for hoarding money for your old age. The woman in the newspaper story proves that you could be needing lots of fancy lawyering, bail money, and liability insurance if you should up and start yanking errant boyfriends' balls off and other stuff like that. Who knows if you're going to act up to that extent? I doubt that anyone *plans* this sort of thing, so you've got to be prepared for the consequences, and they are not cheap.

One of the Queens, Tammy, thinks all women everywhere, no matter what their status—married, single, divorced, employed, being kept in luxury, whatever—should just squirrel money away every chance they get. That's probably the essence of all financial advice you could get from the experts, from Suze Orman on down. When you strip away all the big words and convoluted jargon, it comes down to *"Squirrel money away every chance you get."* And it doesn't matter from whom you are squirreling it. You might be married to a doctor and sitting on your happy ass all day long; squirrel money away in case he decides he'd rather his nurse be sitting on *her* happy ass all day. You might be working night and day—at your own business or at the counter at the Krystal; squirrel money away so you won't *have* to work night and day your whole adult life.

We didn't really think it was necessary to discuss birth control, figuring that Queens are smart enough to have this covered. But just when you think you know somebody, well, they'll up and prove you wrong, wrong, wrong. We read in the paper about a fifty-five-year-old woman—you read right, that's *fifty-five*—who had *quadruplets!* Since the pregnancy was in vitro, it was clearly on purpose. I've got to tell you, we were all pretty happy that we hadn't done this and also that none of us had even considered it. Nor had we considered pulling out all our teeth with the pliers or slamming our fingers in the car door repeatedly just to see what it feels like.

FINANCIAL TIP

If you're going to have a big sack of babies, try to work it into your schedule *before* menopause.

As we've gotten older, food has only gotten more important to us. Friends—our dear *old* friends—have become more important to us as well. So sharing food with friends is now our idea of the ultimate entertainment. The discussion of any gathering immediately raises the questions of "Who all is coming?" and "What are we going to eat?"

The Sweet Potato Queens are in Mal's St. Paddy's Parade the third weekend of each and every March that rolls around, and many other Queens now make the pilgrimage to Jackson, Mississippi, for the parade. So many have joined us that we now call it the Million Queen March, and I believe we'll hit that magic number before too long! (We do love those who come to play with us.) The twentieth anniversary of the parade was in 2002, and it was a banner year.

This was the year that brought NuClia Waste all the way from Denver, Colorado. NuClia did come, NuClia did see, and NuClia did more than conquer. She absolutely *slayed* us all with her radiant beauty. Peyton Prospere and the Buckethead Judges will never be quite the same again, I'm sure. (Of course, that bunch was never "the same" to begin with.) NuClia was around ten feet tall, thanks to the stilts she wore for the entire parade route, and to her hat, which was nearly as big around as she was tall. Tagging along, heeling properly as any well-trained pet should, was the seven-foot (inflatable) reptile Gay-tor.

And NuClia was not only *bee-you-tee-full*, she was an absolute angel to all the other Queens. We simply *must* institute a Miss Congeniality Award and give it to NuClia next year. She even shared her beauty secrets. For instance, if you saw her Saturday night after the parade at the gala at the Crowne Plaza (also known as "Pearls and PJ's"), then you saw NuClia's lovely green hair and you, like me, probably couldn't help but notice that not a hair got out of place *ever*. Our precious, darling George, who was making a rare public appearance as Sue Ellen, was consumed with curiosity about how she achieved this marvel, and NuClia just told, flat out, how to do it, and we are so grateful. NuClia's Secret Weapon Hair Spray is made by diluting Elmer's Glue with water until it will squirt out a spray bottle! Honey, you could hang your head out the car window like a dog and your hair ain't fixin' to move. It was just so sweet of her to tell us. Those of us with four hairs each are eager to try it on our real hair as well.

After NuClia got back to Denver, I had just the sweetest note from her saying that she had a whole new appreciation for Older Women. She used to look around and see Older Women in public, she said, and think, Oh, that poor thing is no longer young and she's no longer having fun. After reading the Sweet Potato Queens books and being in the parade, now when she sees Older Women, she thinks to herself, I wonder how much fun this woman is when she lets loose. I wonder what fun and adventures and stories this woman has in her life. *I wonder what she would look like in a tiara.*

Chocolate Gravy and Biscuits

NuClia sent me some of her absolutely radioactive recipes. One of them, I swear, was for peanut butter cookies that contain not only lard but also ground pork. I swooned when I read it and not in a good way. She confessed that she had never personally made the recipe and suggested that I might want to try it first, but I was sore afraid and couldn't bring myself to embark on such a path at this point in my life. But Chocolate Gravy is another matter altogether! Chocolate Gravy and Biscuits sounds like heaven waiting to happen, does it not? So here's how to make it happen: Mix **3 tablespoons flour, 2 tablespoons Hershey's cocoa** (in the brown box) **a dash of salt,** and **4 tablespoons sugar** in a shallow pan until well-blended. Then add **2 cups milk** and stir. Cook over medium-high heat until it bubbles and thickens, then add **2 tablespoons butter** and **1 running-over teaspoon vanilla** and stir. Open a can of whomp biscuits (those are the ones you have to whomp on the edge of the counter to open), bake them, split the biscuits open, and pour the gravy over 'em. Eat until you're glowing.

Stinky Bread

Now, here's something to help you in the aging process, a recipe given to me aeons ago by my friend Adrienne Hemphill, and guess what the most important ingredient is? Cheese! We always called this Stinky Bread on account of it's both stinky and bread. In a bowl, moosh up **1 cup butter, 1 to 2 cloves garlic, 1¼ tablespoons dried basil,** crushed, **2 tablespoons capers,** rinsed, drained, and chopped up tiny, and **salt** to taste. Stir all that up real good. Okay, now get a **loaf of French bread** (about a foot long) and cut the crust off the top and sides, but leave the bottom alone. Slice the bread almost through at a little less than 1-inch intervals and then put a slice of **mozzarella cheese** in each slot! (You'll need close to *a pound* of cheese for this!) Put the cheese-stuffed loaf on a big sheet of heavy foil and make sort of a little cradle for it (but don't cover the top) and put it on a cookie sheet. Now get that butter goo you made in the beginning and completely cover the top and sides of the loaf with it— just like icing a cake—and then put it in the oven on broil until it's brown and gooey and bubbly. Check it out and if your cheese hasn't melted completely, return it to the oven to bake for a minute or so until the cheese is all melty and delightful. It doesn't matter what you serve after this, nobody will notice. You can serve spaghetti out of a *can* and nobody will care—they're gonna fill up on this, anyway.

Catshit Cookies

An honored member of our Worldwide Sweet Potato Queen Movement, Diana, wrote that she and her friends were taking it easy in their old age (their forties), and they liked to make what they call Catshit Cookies (well, that *is* sort of what they look like) because they don't take any time to make—you don't even have to bake 'em. Just put **1 stick butter,** $1/2$ **cup cocoa, 2 cups sugar,** and $1/2$ **cup milk** in a pan and cook it just until it bubbles a little bit around the sides. Then take it off the heat and dump in **3 cups Quick Oatmeal,** $1/2$ **cup peanut butter,** and **1 running-over teaspoon vanilla.** Stir it up and drop globs of it onto waxed paper and let it cool. (Cooling is, of course, optional.) Diana and her friends' favorite pastime is "water buffaloing": They all lie in the shallow end of the pool and drink. Diana and her friends are aging gracefully, sounds like to me.

The Twelve Steps of Getting Old and Fat

Now, here's a program we've devised for your Old and Fat Ordeal. In order to have any sort of appreciation for these steps, you really have to have some familiarity with the Twelve Steps of Alcoholics Anonymous. It actually wouldn't hurt anybody to spend a little time reading and thinking about those Twelve Steps; they really apply to anything that's messing up your life, be it alcohol or food or relationships or video games. If you know you're spending way too much time, money, and emotional energy on something, chances are you need to apply the Twelve Steps to it. (You can view those steps at www.alcoholicsanonymous.com.)

Getting old and fat is something I can guarantee you is gonna take up a whole bunch of your time, money, and emotional energy, but the original Twelve Steps weren't quite subject-specific enough for me. You can't really stop getting old (there aren't any "recovering old people") except to stop living, and that seems too harsh a remedy even for a malady that sucks as bad as "old" does. Anytime I can't make an actual change in a circumstance, there's not but one thing left to do: make fun of it and try to make fun *out of it*.

So here's a starting point for all of us on the slippery side of forty—our own personal Twelve Steps.

1. We admitted we were powerless over pies and all things tasty and that our hormones, our moods, and our waistlines had become unmanageable.

2. Came to believe that there was no power on earth that could keep us from eating, improve our dispositions, manage our hormones, cause us to enjoy exercise, or sufficiently moisturize our skin.

3. Made a decision to submit a laundry list of miracles (e.g., let me wake up skinny and rich with a gorgeous young stud who adores me) to God, as we understood Him, and beg Him to perform them on our behalf—with no effort on our part whatsoever.

4. Made a searching and fearless physical, moral, and financial inventory of everybody we know (in hopes of feeling better about ourselves by finding at least *one* person who's a bigger mess than we are).

5. Admitted to God, to ourselves, and to our closest, dearest, most intimate girlfriend the exact number of pounds registering on the scales, minus eight.

6. Were entirely ready to have God—and/or our medical and cosmetic professionals—remove all the excess poundage, gray hair, mood swings, and wrinkles.

7. Begged Him on bended knee to do so, and while He was at it, to bestow all of these things on our enemies.

8. Made a list of all persons currently thin and became willing to make them a pie and/or a cheese ball—anything in order to put a few pounds on them.

9. Made pies personally for such people whenever possible except when Sara Lee had a special on ready-made pecan pies, in which case we bought them by the crate and distributed them liberally.

10. Continued to monitor the lives of everyone we know and advise them at every opportunity (who knows better than *us* what *they* should be doing, and it distracts us from our own situations so nicely).

11. Sought through constant conversations over coffee and pie (and/or margaritas and Armadillo Dip, depending largely on the time of day) to find the name of any doctor on the planet who might have some clue as to what to do about our hormones and, barring that, the name of a really good plastics guy—knowing, as we do, that in this world, it is a far, far better thing to look good than to feel good.

12. Having come to the realization that we're all gonna wrinkle up and die one day anyway, resolved to have as much fun as possible on every single day left to us and to exhort others to eat some pie and join us in this pursuit.

We offer these Twelve Steps as a guide—suggestions, as it were—for twenty-something-year-old people who have awakened to find themselves trapped in forty- or fifty- or even more-something bodies.

Knowing, as we do, that Acceptance is the Key to all our problems, we suggest that the purchase of two good mirrors (one full-length and one with at least a 5× magnification) is in order. Get yourself in front of these and just *deal* with it. We *know* you feel like a sweet, young thing, but you're not—you're probably just about as far past sweet as you are past young. We *know* that when hip-huggers were in style before you could have taught Britney a thing or two about belly buttons—and dancing, too, for that matter.

But That, as they say, was Then, and This, as they further insist, Is Now. and ne'er the twain shall meet. And it doesn't matter. Even if by some bizarre twist of good fortune you still can fit into those hip-huggers, *don't wear them out in public* even on Halloween as a joke. Your turn is over—as Britney's will be as well in short order. There's some comfort in that, anyway.

FINANCIAL TIP

Rich old people are generally more attractive than poor old people, so by all means, try to *get* rich *before* age sets in. Otherwise, you'll just be playing catch-up for the rest of your life and that will just wear you out, let me tell you.

Now, here's one recipe you can count on through your Twelve-Step days, and it will carry you sweetly on into your twilight years (it's easy to chew) as well. But be careful or you'll launch yourself right into Overeaters Anonymous.

My good friend Kathy Cohen sent me this recipe with the note that it was good for funerals and potluck "ordeals" (a good description, I thought, and Lord knows you'll be having plenty of those with your fellow Twelve Steppers). "If you're lucky," she added, "no one will eat any and you'll not only get credit for bringing it but get to take it right back home and eat it all yourself." (She sounds smart, doesn't she, and she did show remarkable good sense when she married my friend Edward, but she apparently used it all up on that move, because when it comes to her dogs, she has no sense at all. Just wait till you read one of the funniest books in the history of the world, which she's writing about her life with those crazy dogs of hers—it just shows how people can fool you.)

Kathy's Nobody~Else~in~Venice~Beach~ Cooks~Like~This Jell~O

Get a **big thing of cream cheese** and cut it up in little pieces and let it sit out so it gets soft and will melt real easy. You want **2 packs of Jell-O,** 1 green and 1 yellow (off to a flying start). Just make the Jell-O according to the directions on the box, then put the mooshy cream cheese pieces in there and stir 'em around and mash 'em against the side of the bowl until they get pretty small. Add **1 can sweetened condensed milk** (always a welcome addition), **1 20-ounce can crushed pineapple,** and **1 heaping teaspoon mayonnaise.** Stir it all up, dump it in a Bundt pan, and put it in the refrigerator until it sets. That's the only problem with Jell-O–based food: It's really not gratifying to eat it immediately. I hope you made two, because you know you're gonna eat all of this one.

4

Snip, Snip, Snip and Tra~la~la

After years of yammering about it, I looked hard at myself in the mirror one day and found that my eyeballs were nearly obscured between the enormous bags underneath and the bloodhoundlike folds above, and I just called The Man and made an appointment. Every city's got one—The Man who "does" everybody's "work." The Man in Jackson, Mississippi, would be Dr. David Segrest. There's a reason for this, naturally: He's reeeeally good, and he's also an ophthalmologist, so you feel he won't sacrifice the actual working functions of your eyes in favor of making them *look* good. In most areas, we would come down on the side of "looking good" as opposed to just about anything else. But if forced to choose between eyes that look great and eyes that work—alerting you to the presence of walls and other obstacles—we would have to make the cosmetic sacrifice. And that's why David Segrest does our eyes.

Dr. Segrest is a very congenial sort and we got along famously—which is always a good thing. You definitely do not want any antipathy in the surgical suite, if you know what I mean. He agreed that I possibly needed a "little something" done—I think this is his very diplomatic way of saying, "Good God—you got here *just* in time, and let's pray that nobody thinks I've already worked on you." We scheduled the procedure and I left and proceeded to broadcast the happy news of my pending improvements far and wide—pretty much to anybody who would listen, interested or not. My theory on this kind of thing has always been: People Will Know and People Will Talk, but if I tell it first, at least they can't Talk Behind My Back, and that robs the news of any power. It's hardly a juicy secret if *I* have blabbed it, now is it?

But I should qualify this. I had been telling everybody who got within three feet of me *except* for my Significant Other, the Cutest Boy in the World—Cutie Pie, as my friends all call him. (Well, there was one other person, but that's another story.) I definitely and deliberately did *not* mention it to him. Not out of vanity. It was out of fear and dread. I knew he would pitch a fit about my having "unnecessary" surgery, the risks and so on. Now, I'm willing to admit it was *elective* surgery, but *unnecessary?* Hardly! My eye situation was so bad, I was probably only days away from qualifying for insurance. I looked like one of those wrinkly Chinese dogs; I swear I did. So I didn't tell Cutie Pie because I didn't want to have to listen to him fuss about it. Believing as I do that it is always easier to get forgiveness than permission, I kept my little secret until, well, around four-thirty A.M. on the very day that my surgery was scheduled for ten A.M.

Cutie Pie was getting up early that day to drive back home to Alabama, and I had been awakened, no doubt by my guilty conscience, at around three and I'd been lying there, wrestling in my mind with the whole "tell/don't tell" quandary. About the time his alarm went off, it came to me clear as a bell that he would be furious, perhaps beyond repair, if I did something this significant without telling him. And wouldn't it be awkward if my friends had to call and tell him I died or something equally bizarre? So I put my hand on his arm and said, haltingly, "There's something I've just got to tell you." He collapsed back onto the bed, obviously filled with foreboding. After much hemming and hawing and general stalling, until he was positively out of his mind with curiosity/terror, I finally managed to force the words past my lips: "I'm having my eyes done at ten o'clock this morning." Well, by this time he was so relieved, he was giddy.

He said his first thought had been that I was pregnant—which, given my age, is a distinct compliment, bless his heart, and made me love him even more. Then he thought I was dying or breaking up with him! Or all three. I was pregnant and dying, and since I was already screwed (so to speak), why not ditch him and sow a bucket of wild oats on my way out? That's some pretty convoluted thinking, even for a guy—and all done in the space of the maybe thirty to forty-eight seconds it took me to actually get my announcement out.

Now, even though he had already been up here for over a week recuperating from an injury and he needed to get back to work in the worst way, what do you think he did? Of course. He stayed to take care of me—would a Queen have a lesser man? So off we went to the surgical center, to be met in the parking lot by one of the Queens, Tammy. She was all in a dither on my behalf—so very excited, like I was getting a new fur coat or something. She couldn't wait to see how it was gonna turn out, since we have all been dying to have plastic surgery for at least a couple of years.

Tammy and Cutie Pie hung out with me in the little holding pen until they took me away to go "Under the Knife," as our Southern Mothers have been wont to say. It's never just a hernia repair or a small cyst removed or anything minor-sounding. It's always "I went Under the Knife" or "This will be the third time she's gone Under the Knife." Anyway, they stayed by my side until I left to go Under, and then, naturally, they went out to eat. Luckily, they only had to go just across the street to Keifer's (our favorite neighborhood eatery, owned by Paula Coe and Rick Olson, two of our favorite people), where they have enough feta cheese to soothe even the insatiable soul of Tammy, self-confessed and steadily practicing cheesaholic.

Now, while they were out filling up on feta, I was having a most pleasant surgical experience. This was due, no doubt, to the fabulous drugs they pumped into me. I was sort of semi-awake and all I could feel (besides my body floating like a little wisp of nothingness) was Dr. Segrest very lightly fooling with my face. It was like a facial that's so good, you almost go completely to sleep during it. I swear I was disappointed when it was over! It seemed to have taken about ten minutes, but it actually lasted two hours. Those are some mighty fine drugs is all I'm saying.

So the next thing I know, I'm in the recovery area and Cutie Pie and Tammy are there, all happy and well fed, just billing and cooing over me, as both are inclined to do. The sweet nurse gave Cutie Pie these funny little silicone eye-mask thingies that you put in ice water to get cold as a Witch's Other Elbow (that's what my daddy said instead of the common "tit") and then put on your eyes to keep the swelling down. They were thin and molded completely to the affected area and felt like very cold snot, actually. The sweet nurse told Cutie Pie that the more often you put on a cold one and the longer you kept up this treatment, the better off you'd be. She also gave me a very fine pill and she gave Cutie Pie a little slip of paper, redeemable at any pharmacy for more very fine pills, and she sent us on our merry way.

I was completely happy, having successfully emerged from Under the Knife and being still heavily drugged. Cutie Pie loaded my happy ass into the car and bundled me off home, whereupon I was met by my horrified Mother—the only other person in the Southeast to be totally unaware that surgery was planned. I had gone Under the Knife without telling my own personal Mother, who lives in my very house with me! I just came rolling merrily in and presented my face for her inspection, with no preamble whatsoever. Here I am—I've been gone all day long without so much as a phone call—and I come waltzing deliriously into the house with two shiners and a bunch of stitches.

Mother immediately assumes that I've been in a horrible automobile accident and gone through the windshield, and she's looking past me to Cutie Pie, who is completely unscathed, and she's wondering, Where are *his* injuries? She didn't verbalize this, of course, but you could tell she was hunting for the guilty and she believed she had found him. All the way home from the clinic I had threatened Cutie Pie: "I'm gonna go in and show Mama my face and tell her that I found out I was pregnant, and when I told you, you beat the crap out of me, but we spent the day in the emergency room and made up and that you're moving in and we're gonna be needing her room for the baby!" He was pretty scared.

She was not at all prepared for me to come in and announce that I had been Under the Knife and out again before she even got to worry a single minute, and I wasn't making much sense trying to explain it. After some while, Mama finally relaxed and accepted that it was a done deal and that Cutie Pie had nothing to do with it. Why, he would have lobbied as hard as she to prevent it, if he had just been given the chance. What really won Mama's heart, though, was the way Cutie Pie took care of me during my convalescence.

Remember those little cold packs I told you the nurse said should be frequently changed and used for a long time? Well, Cutie Pie took her instructions plumb to heart, he did, and stayed up all night for two whole nights, changing those cold thingies on my face every fifteen minutes. I'm laid out, mouth-breathing, snoring my medicated self away, and he's on the couch in the den, with a new cold thingie in a bowl of ice cubes, ready to swap out the one on my face at every commercial break in whatever dreadful late-night show he was watching on TV. Only when I woke up—or rather came to—the next morning and was able to change them for myself would he get in bed and go to sleep. But not before instructing me sternly that I was to continue with his fifteen-minute cycle. He was not staying up all night changing those things only to have *me* slack off and swell up because of it. I did as I was told, figuring it probably was the least I could do for him. If there's anything a Queen is interested in doing, it's the *least* amount possible.

Needless to say, not only is Mama totally in love with him for it—how can you *not* love somebody who takes good care of your baby?—but Dr. Segrest was flabbergasted when I presented myself for stitch removal the next week. You could hardly tell I'd had surgery, so unswollen was I. When I told him about Cutie Pie's forty-eight-hour ice-pack vigil, he said you couldn't even *buy* nursing that good, and I said it would never have occurred to me to *ask* somebody to do that for me—even for large sums of money. I mean, from what place in yourself do you come up with "How's about *you* stay up all night long for a couple of nights and put this cold stuff on my face, oh, say, every fifteen minutes while I take drugs and sleep?" Even I, True Queen that I am, couldn't bring myself to make the Promise with a straight face for this kind of service. But was I glad to get it? You betcha! (Oops, I meant to say "Boy hidee!" My dear friend Bruce "Perhaps I Can Help" Browning possesses a violent distaste for the Midwestern "you betcha" and I vowed to help reeducate folks to substitute the utterly bewildering Southern "boy hidee.")

I'm thrilled with the way my eyes turned out. I have actual eyelids for the first time in I don't know how long, and the whole experience was so entirely satisfactory that I frequently find myself in front of the mirror pondering, What's next? I'm on a plastic surgery roll now, I'm ready for the works. One of the Queens—I'm sure it was Tammy—and I have often discussed having liposuction done, but we could never decide which fat to have removed first. What we really want is for them to just cut a hole in the top of our heads and start sucking! They're gonna need a big pump and a lot of time, too.

The Pluperfect Brownie

When one is laid up recuperating from going Under the Knife, one's friends should hop to and make one some of these brownies to speed one's recovery. I got this recipe (and, even more important, some of these brownies) from my friend Ann Coe. Melt together **6 tablespoons Hershey's cocoa** (in the brown box) and **2 sticks plus 2 tablespoons butter** (just the right amount, don't you think?). Then mix together **2 eggs** and **2 cups sugar**. Add the cocoa-butter to that and then add **1 running-over teaspoon vanilla**, **1 cup flour**, **¼ teaspoon salt**, and **1 cup pecans**. Grease up the lucky brownie pan and bake at 300 for 45 to 55 minutes. Ann says to cool them for an hour before eating—but, of course, you know what we say to that: tee-hee.

FINANCIAL TIP

Plastic surgery is no place to scrimp. It is worth exactly what you pay for it, which is plenty. Get the money somehow—*any* how. Do not hesitate to borrow money for plastic surgery. Put it on a designated credit card or, hey, get a home improvement loan. You, after all, are the most important thing in your home, and no matter what, once you get it, it's yours—it cannot be repossessed.

5

Exercise, Diet, and Other Cheesy Ideas

The Tammys and I have become semi-survivalists. I say "semi" in that we aren't really into building forts and hoarding supplies and all that. Actually, we've been eating all the supplies and we aren't even interested in a fort unless it's got good books and silk sheets and excellent air-conditioning and five or so stars after its name. So I guess what I'm saying is that we aren't really survivalists, semi or otherwise, except that I read somewhere that fat people live longer through a famine, and so, just in case there is one, we are becoming big, fat pigs. But we're having a Fine Time.

Grilled Bologna Po~Boy

Our friend Tom Massey taught us how to make a grilled bologna po-boy that is to die for, if not from. Disgusting food items vary from region to region in this country. For example, most of us in the South consider bratwurst to be inedible and singularly unattractive, but the way people in Wisconsin eat it, you'd think it's sugar dumplin's. On the other hand, you would be hard pressed to find a pure Southerner who has *not*, at some time in his or her life, happily consumed a fried bologna sandwich (pronounced "baloney sammich")—although in recent years it's become increasingly difficult to get some of them to admit it. Nonetheless, we know it to be true and Tom has managed to put somewhat of a gourmet twist, if you will, on this regional staple. He uses really **high-quality balogna** (if that's not an oxymoron, there never was one) and he grills it with **purple onions.** (We find that just about any food that doesn't actually contain chocolate can probably be improved by the addition of some grilled purple onions.) He then puts it on some excellent **French bread** and melts a big wad of **Pepper Jack** and **Cheddar cheese** on it. (Note: Foods that are improved by grilled purple onions are generally also improved by big wads of cheese.) This is one fine sammich, I am here to tell you.

My dear friend Larry L. (*Best Little Whorehouse in Texas*) King was bemoaning, via e-mail, the state of his own personal physical fitness or rather the total lack thereof, and I revealed to him that in a former life I had been a fitness professional, known in some parts of the country as a "personal trainer." In horror he wrote back:

> *I knew you were too damned good to be true: all this time you've been a secret fitness freak and your whole purpose in making me Promises and other exotic offers for adventures has been to trick me into running nine miles per day, walking an additional twelve miles, doing thirty push-ups per hour, carrying heavy objects for the alleged fun in it, chasing birds and squirrels, taking cold showers and running in place while I cleanse myself. You also want me to sleep on a cold floor, alone and without a pallet. I am to get up at 4:30 A.M. to begin my roadwork, and may breakfast only on prunes (lots of prunes!). Lunch is to be cauliflower, asparagus, broccoli and turnips. Dinner shall be soy beans and seaweed and raw octopus—or even worse, octopui. When not doing all of the above, I shall sit in the Zen Buddhist position and hum and chant. If I even touch my privates, my face will break out. If I think Impure Thoughts, my dingus will fall off. Wednesday nights I am to go to Church of Christ Prayer Meeting, where I cannot even have music with my hymns. I must, of course, run there and back and each time you will set the dogs on me. Each night, some strange man with hairy legs and a big nose and bulbous lips and body odor will come to my house and curse me to sleep while flailing me with a cat-o-nine*

tails. Length of Fitness Program: the rest of my life plus nineteen days.

A Fitness Professional! Jesus Christ! What have I DID to deserve this? And you seemed like such a nice girl!

I wondered aloud as I read it if maybe he'd secretly been in contact with some of my former clients—the Whiners and Slackasses? As most of us know, getting in shape may not be easy, but it is simple. I never tire, while standing in the grocery-store checkout line, of reading the magazine and tabloid head-lines that make all manner of promises to that effect. For just a few dollars, one can learn who's gained/lost weight, how much and how they did it, good or bad (as well as more than one could ever want to know about even one's closest friends, let alone perfect strangers in far-off places—who is doing what, to and with whom, and how everybody else is reacting to it, who said what about whom and who is filing a lawsuit as a result, what everybody's wearing to which big-deal event—it's all there in black, white, and Technicolor).

I recently saw this headline, FIT INTO YOUR THIN CLOTHES! LOSE A WHOLE SIZE *WITHOUT* DIETING! GET RESULTS IN 14 DAYS THE WAY CELEBRITIES DO! Now, I ask you, who could resist such a teasing line? Eight exercises were described, and we were *promised* that if we do these and only these (no dieting!), and do them three to four times a week, well, in fourteen days we will be a whole size smaller. Mercy! How good is that?

Here's a synopsis of this Miracle Disappearing Act. First, the warm-up. You stand on your right foot, lifting your left knee and your right hand simultaneously, pulling the knee in close to your chest, using the leg muscles (only no fair helping with your other hand—they're very strict!). You alternate sides and do this 25 times on each side.

Next you do an exercise that promises to "lengthen" your legs. At nearly six feet one I was somewhat aghast at the prospect, but here's what they said to do: Holding on to a chair with your left hand, turn your toes out and put your heels together. Lift your heels and then lower your body down to knee level, pressing the heels together and holding for 10 seconds. Then they want you to bounce up and down. They didn't say how many times. But they want you to return to the start position after the bouncing and repeat the procedure 10 to 15 times. My own personal knees went into absolute convulsions at the mere reading of that exercise. I would not do it on a bet, but if there are any starving orthopedic surgeons out there, I bet they're praying that we all do it and do it a lot.

Next is your chest. This calls for 25 to 30 reps of what amounts to a push-up done with your hands on the back of a chair and your body stretched out an incline. If you do this, pray mightily that the chair does not flip over and knock out all your teeth.

After your chest, they target your triceps by having you do triceps kickbacks with a one-pound weight, 25 times with each arm. (Apparently, they thought your back and biceps are already perfect—there are no exercises for them!)

Exercise, Diet, and Other Cheesy Ideas

You can magically transform your hips by standing on your left foot and extending your right leg out and back to the side, then lifting that leg up, doing a little squeeze/hold thing, and returning to the start positions. Only 20 reps to each side will do the trick.

Your behind will be shrunk to the size of a tiny baby lima if only you will lie on the floor, knees bent, and slowly raise your hips off the floor while tucking your pelvis in and pressing your shoulders back. You will need to do this 10 times slow and 10 times fast. What makes this work, they say, is the pressing of your shoulders—who'da thunk it?

You're probably currently unaware—as I was—that to get those washboard abs, all you have to do is sit on the floor, with your knees drawn up to your chest, hands under your knees, and just round your back into a C shape 25 times and presto—no more gut for you!

The very last exercise promised to lengthen your entire body (again, I shuddered) if you just bend forward with your hands on the back of that chair and extend your left leg back in a lunge position and hold it for 10 to 12 seconds. You'll be needing 6 to 8 reps of this one for each leg to maximize your length.

I swear, if you can do these silly exercises (and nothing else—no aerobics, no dieting, no weight lifting) and lose a size in fourteen days, well, I don't know what I'll do, but I'll think of something appropriately ridiculous. The very idea!

Do not ever buy one of these magazines for these stupid exercise tips. *Do* buy them, however, for the unretouched photos of celebrities going out to the grocery store like regular people and looking like—guess what?—*regular people*, meaning like something the cat's been sucking on for a day or two. Look at them when you need reminding that our goal is *progress*, not *perfection*, and until we can all get airbrushed, we'll just have to settle for it.

Or you can get real happy about being real fat—like the guy I read about in the paper who was so fat he got stuck in his bathroom door. There's something you want to get in the paper for! There was also a running list of what he customarily eats in one day. Now, on a given day, I can put away some groceries, and on some days, I'd just as soon nobody really *know* just how much I eat, but I've got to say, I felt a lot better about my occasional bag of chips when I read this guy's list: five chickens (whole chickens, not pieces of), twelve pounds of pork chops, three loaves of bread, six dozen eggs, eight gallons of ice cream, and a carrot! I do think he's a little light on the leafy greens.

That one carrot just killed me, but it did give me pause for thought. Whenever any diet guru talks to us about moderation, I just have to laugh. Everybody's moderate when it comes to stuff like oatmeal and beets and sprouts—that's the easiest thing in the world to do. It is simply not a problem to restrain my desire to consume lettuce. Brussels sprouts? Put a vatful of 'em right smack in front of me—they're safe, I'm telling you. I can eat steamed vegetables with the decorum of a food saint—no rush, no gulping, really no need for a napkin even. It's pie (and the like) that sets me off in a feeding frenzy. Stuff that's only got about twenty-five calories in a pound is not a threat to my moderation quotient. It's when you get into the triple digits that I get in trouble.

And here's something else I've noticed: We all judge other people's behavior/choices based on *our own ability to resist.* For example, a dear friend of mine is a recovering alcoholic, and she just doesn't understand drug addicts at all. She can resist heroin all day long, doesn't care if they quit making it, means nothing to her. Jack Daniel's, on the other hand—now, there's something she can identify with, and it's exceedingly difficult for her to imagine how anybody can resist ole Jack.

You can see this principle in action in the grocery-store checkout line. You'll see the ones who are Not Sweets Eaters (poor blighted individuals) casting positively scathing looks at the purchasers of Sara Lee and her buddies. But then, at the same time, the Sweets Eaters will be horrified by the people buying every kind of chip made in this country today. Then you have people like, say, me, who are eating all over the map. I've got it all in there—sweet, salty, crispy, gooey, cheesy—and throw in a little lemon-something just to cleanse the palate. Foodies can't understand why drunks don't just give it up and have a little something to eat. The drunks don't care if there's a worldwide famine, as long as there's some grain fermenting somewhere. The druggies don't mind the famine either, as long as it doesn't affect the poppy crop. The point, of course, is that we all think that those other people would be just fine if *they* could only exercise a little moderation.

But back to the Really Fat Guy. According to the paper, he

got off his triple-king-sized bed only to go to the bathroom (and thanks be to mercy that he did). What I want to know is who is the mindless twit holed up in the kitchen all damn day cooking all that crap for this lard bucket—hmmmm? And will he or she (or they) kindly relocate to Mississippi? I mean, I get a picture of the pitiful specimen slaving in a kitchen—round the clock, I'm talking—for Mr. Two Tons of Buns in there stuck in the bathroom door, for crying out loud. How in this world does he get them to do all that cooking?

And how does he afford it, since he's too fat to get out of bed, let alone go to work? Is the guy so independently wealthy he can afford to be the fattest, laziest slug on the face of the earth, and his poor blighted sister cooks her little heart out for him day after day, just waiting for him to fat to death and praying he doesn't eat up her inheritance? Well, whatever, I wish I had his job and he had a black pudding on his nose.

I guess I should explain that black pudding thing. When I was little, Daddy used to tell me the story of an old man and an old woman and how one day, for some good deed, the old man was awarded three wishes by a grateful fairy. He was hungry at that moment and, thinking only of his own immediate gratification, he quickly wished for a black pudding. (Daddy never explained—if in fact he even knew—what a black pudding was, but I surmised it was highly desirable since the guy used a whole wish on one.) And quick as anything—*poof!*—there appeared before the man a black pudding. Well, his wife, seeing so quickly as she did the absolute folly of wasting a whole wish on something of so little lasting value, flew into a rage. And she also quickly and without much, if any, forethought and, as I envisioned, through clenched teeth, shrieked, "You idiot, I wish you had that black pudding on your *nose!*" And *poof!* Every bit as quickly as the pudding had appeared, it magically transported itself to the old man's nose, where it hung, I always imagined, like a wet flag on a windless day. In vain horror, the old man tried to remove it. He pulled and he pulled and he pu-u-u-u-ullled, but it would not budge; he still had a black pudding on his nose, and from all appearances, it was there to stay. And so-o-o-o, predictably, they had to use their third and final wish to wish the dang thing off his nose. The predictable moral is: Be careful what you wish for, on account of you just might get it. Daddy used it, however, when he wanted to express mild envy; not wanting to wish something for himself and nothing for the other person, he would say that *he* wished he had *that*, and *the other person* had a black pudding on his nose.

Big-Ass Cheese Dip

Just in case you *are* the person cooking for that really fat guy— here's a recipe for a whole big lot of cheese dip. The Library Club Queens who sent this called it Asiago Cheese Dip, but we prefer to think of it as Big-Ass Cheese Dip. Start off by getting **3 pounds of sundried tomatoes** (the kind in oil) and reconstituting them in hot water. Then dry 'em off a bit and cut 'em up into fine strips—julienne them, if you will. Then make a big pile of about quarter-inch slices of **8 pounds of green onions** and slice up **5 pounds of mushrooms**. Mix together **4 gallons of may-**

onnaise, **4 gallons of sour cream,** and **6 pounds of shredded Asiago cheese,** and add the onions and mushrooms. Add the tomatoes last and just stir it up till it's blended well. Then, when you're ready to eat it, heat all of that—but don't bring it to a boil. Eat it on French bread or toasted bread rounds or *any-thing*—your fingers would be fine. It does make a nice vatful, doesn't it?

Heaven on a Cracker

This recipe was sent to us by our favorite SPQ Wannabe, Queen Kimmydarling, boss queen of the Larva Queens: They're under forty and therefore, in my opinion, larva. Amongst ourselves, we call it the Larva Dip, but that conjures up an icky mental picture, so we just named it Heaven on a Cracker. The proportions of this one are slightly more manageable for everyday use. Soften **16 ounces Philadelphia cream cheese** in the microwave. (I'd take it out of that foil wrapper first if I were you.) Then combine that with ⅔ **cup Miracle Whip** (Kimmydarling says nothing else will do here—she's already tried substituting all different kinds of mayo and it screws it up, so learn from her experience), **8 ounces shredded Swiss cheese,** and **1 to 3 table-spoons green onion,** finely chopped (I like green onions myself, so I use closer to three). Mix it all together and put it in a micro-wave-safe dish. Then stir up **16 slices of cooked, crumbled bacon** (which means you will have cooked 32 and eaten half of it already) with **1 sleeve Ritz crackers,** crushed. Put that delightful mixture on top of the cheesy stuff and nuke it on high until it gets hot all the way through (depending on your microwave, shouldn't take more than 2 to 3 minutes) and serve it with tortilla chips, crackers, or, of course, Fritos. I like this one best with Ritz crackers my ownself. Is it any wonder why Kimmydarling is such a favorite of ours?

FINANCIAL TIP

If you spend enough money on diet books, exercise equipment that either doesn't work (because it's crap) or can't work (because you never touch it), diet "aids" you drink, chew, or wear on your wrist (none of which will work), and joining gyms and exercise classes you never go to, eventually you will not have enough money to buy actual food and you will lose weight—at last.

6

Career Opportunities for Big~Ass Bucks

Every day it seems we hear of yet another career niche we wish we'd thought of—indeed, that we are kicking ourselves for having *not* thought of first. Several years ago, it was the whole trance-channeling thing where people paid gazillions of dollars to hear the inane babblings of people who allegedly lived thirty-five thousand years ago and had unexpectedly decided to pop in and out of the bodies of a few randomly selected average persons currently numbering among the living. My sister, Judy, and I could have "trance-channeled" our dead daddy with total confidence that he would have made more sense than any of those dead guys, and we would have happily done it for, oh, say, *half* a gazillion dollars. Folks would have saved a heap of cash and gotten some usable advice for their trouble and money.

Recently we have noted with interest the trendy new job of Lifestyle Coach. This is somebody (who received on-line training from the absolute genius who thought it up) you pay five hundred dollars an hour to tell you what, in their opinion, it is you ought to do in any given situation. Oh, hey, is this job made for me, or what? I *always* know what *other* people ought to be doing in any given situation. Always. I can't think of an exception right offhand. And here, all my adult life, I've been telling everybody what they ought to be doing in any given situation, and I've been doing it for free. And what's more, they didn't even have to ask me what, in my opinion, they ought to be doing. My sister has been providing the same service for all of her friends and acquaintances as well—and likewise, unsolicited and gratis. We are considering billing them all retroactively. They are seriously in arrears—and getting further behind every day, since we have not slowed down in dispensing advice.

Some careers, I'm afraid, we'll have to chalk up as Missed Opportunities. We are way too old to take up plastic surgery. Talk about your Growth Industry! With all these baby-boomers hitting menopause—get outta here! We're so old now, it's probably too late for us to even go to beauty school. But hey, here's something we could do: *plastic surgery consulting.* This is just a further extension of our other coaching (butting-in) duties. We can look at *anybody* and tell them instantly what "work" they ought to have done and how soon they ought to think about it, too. We could just sit in beauty shops, grocery stores, and gyms, snagging passers-by, offering them the benefit of our observations, and directing them to the appropriate professional—who would, in turn, pay us a finder's fee.

With everybody getting fatter and more desperate about it with every passing minute, we are not at all surprised at the wide range of opportunities in wildly expensive boondoggles related to the fitness industry. One of our favorites is a place out west that has been visited by many high-profile persons in the public eye—including one of our very own Queens, Tammy. For approximately five thousand to ten thousand dollars a week (depending on whether you want to share a bathroom with just one other person or several), you get to stay in what was formerly somebody's fairly small ranch-style house; absolutely no modifications have been done on it to make it spalike in any way—it's just a dumpy little house, period.

There you can get up at five every morning to hike eight or nine miles up a big hill, at the top of which you are given *one half* of an orange. Then you hike the same eight or nine miles back down the big hill, at the bottom of which they give you the *other half* of your orange. Then you go do a little yoga or some other exercise and have lunch, which is like hot water and a carrot, and then you do some more moving around and they give you your dinnertime ration of the hot water–carrot thing. After "dinner," you go to bed in your room that you share with at least one other person—depending on how much more than the basic five thousand you paid. You don't have a phone in your room and there's no maid service. I swear this is a real place and real people go there—a lot of 'em—and pay big bucks to do it.

I wish you would just consider the profit margin of running such an establishment out of *your* house. Let's say you have four bedrooms and it was a week without any Big Spenders, so you've got four people in each room at five thousand dollars a head, and all you're feeding them is slightly more than one entire orange a day each. I am *so* doing this next summer. Come to my house, all ye with more money and body weight than sense, and I will personally get your asses out of bed at five A.M. each and every day and tell you to walk out to the ten-mile marker, where you will each be met with your half an orange, before you turn around and walk ten miles back for the other half. If you don't make it back, don't worry about your fellow inmates getting your orange, I'll eat it my ownself. But there will be no refunds. You will be by-God skinny by the time you leave and I'll be rich as a nabob.

One day, after we get all our kids out of college and have completed all the plastic surgery on ourselves that needs to be done, we want to wind up all together on some wonderful beach. Over the years, we've talked about it extensively and we've come up with some great plans for income-producing establishments—cash cows, if you will—that would require only minimal work on our part but max out in the payday department, naturally.

Tammy Carol and I want to open a Krispy Kreme doughnut shop in Cancun; one of us would be willing to go in the store once or twice a day but only when the "hot" sign is on and really only to get doughnuts for ourselves. For the uninitiated, bless your heart, a Krispy Kreme is the Best Doughnut Ever in the History of the Entire World, Living or Dead. I am not exaggerating. I can drive through and get a dozen hot ones and they'll be completely gone before I've gone a mile. I am powerless over Krispy Kremes—a serving for me is however many there are. If you don't have Krispy Kreme doughnuts where you live, drop us a line; we'll come open one in your town, too. We like to think of it as missionary work. (And after you've eaten enough of 'em, you can sign up for my "spa-in-my-house.")

Tammy Pippa wants to open a bait shop and sell bait, obviously, and the absolute coldest beer in town, and we're all for it, because we all know who wants bait and the absolute coldest beer in town, don't we? But Tammy Donna's establishment will be the one where we'll spend most of our time. Oh yeah, we'll all be hanging out at the Bitch Bar. It will be an oceanside affair with lots of comfy chairs and fabulous views of the sunrise and sunset and many, many ceiling fans. Only music we are in the mood to hear will ever be playing. It will have low (face-flattering) lighting at all times of day. Anybody we are not in the mood for will have to leave. Everybody else is welcome. We will greet everyone as they arrive, if we feel like it right then. The bar will contain everything to make every variation of fruity drink anybody could possibly dream up. We won't actually wait on anybody—ever. We will sit around in our comfy chairs, and if somebody wants something and speaks to us about it, we'll look up and snarl (bitchlike) and say, *"There's* the *bar*—fix it yourself!" And then we'll bitch at 'em for using too much liquor or making a mess or something. And we'll talk bad about 'em— as if it were behind their backs, but it won't be because they'll be right there. Anybody who's got a complaint about anything in the world outside the Bitch Bar can bring it up for discussion and we will all bitch about it with them till we just wear it slap out. Anybody who's got a complaint about anything *in* or *about* the Bitch Bar can just shut the hell up about it, and get happy, or not, we don't care—it's the shutting-up part that matters.

No one wearing a cute outfit or makeup will be allowed in—only big, giant T-shirts, baggy shorts, muumuus, and untweezed eyebrows will be permitted. If *anybody's* allowed to be cute, *everybody* will feel pressured to be cute, so cute's out, comfy's in. If you are one of those heinously annoying people who can manage to be cute and comfy, you will be let in but only so we can maim you, cut big random hunks out of your hair, and mess up your outfit. Tammy Melanie and Tammy Donna are pretty adamant that nobody with good hair be allowed in, and I'm inclined to go along with 'em on this; it will only ruin our dispositions if we have to deal with hair-envy in our own bar. But I came up with an acceptable compromise: If we are in a good humor, we will wear our big red wigs; we are not threatened by *any* head of hair when we are wearing those. If we are feeling a trifle crabby and don't feel like having our wigs on, then anybody showing up with good hair will be required to stuff it up in a tight white bathing cap, which we will happily provide. This in itself may make us cheerful enough to go put on our red wigs. There will be a nap room. Absolutely, positively *no* children will be allowed—by this we mean no one under forty, obviously.

If your dress size is below an eight, you won't be allowed in. If you are actually a size fourteen but can manage to squeeze your lardass into a four so that the pockets and pleats are stretched wide open and flat, you can drink and eat for free because you will make us feel so much better about our own lardasses. Well, if you're a genuine tight six, you can come in if you promise to eat and drink a whole lot, thereby demonstrating your good intent to pork up.

Bitch Bacon Bread Sticks

You might order the Bitch Bacon Bread Sticks, for example. We will cause these to be made for you in this manner: Someone (not us personally) will preheat the oven at the Bitch Bar to 350 and then take some very thinly sliced **bacon** out of the fridge (they're gonna need **about 30 slices** of bacon) and let it sit for about 10 minutes to soften up. Then our cook will get a **box of grissini** (those long, skinny bread sticks) and very carefully wrap one of those thin slices of bacon around each long, skinny bread stick in a delightful spiral of fat. Then this same busy person will mix together ⅓ **cup dark brown sugar** and **3 tablespoons chili powder** in a long, shallow dish (long enough to lay a bread stick down in) and smash out any lumps with a fork and generally mix it all up real good. Then the dear one in the kitchen will ever so gently roll each bacon-wrapped bread stick in that hot sugar and set them, one by one, on the rack of a broiler pan, about $^1/_2$ inch apart, and then bake them for about 20 minutes—during which time that sugar will caramelize in the bacon fat and the bacon will turn wonderfully golden. They'll then be loosened with a spatula and cooled on that rack on the counter for a few minutes before they they are placed on a serving platter, but that's okay—you want to eat 'em at room temp, anyway.

Bitch Bar Bacon Swimps

And then, if you think you need just a le-e-etle bit more bacon to make your quota for the day, try these shrimp (or swimps, as some of us like to call them down here). For Bitch Bar Bacon Swimps, get a bunch of thin-sliced **bacon** and cook it until it's almost but not quite done, either in a frying pan or the microwave—doesn't matter. Get some big, giant **shrimps**—if possible, from some place like Sal and Phil's in Jackson, where they will peel, devein, and butterfly them for you so you don't have to do it yourself. Then put a hunk of **Pepper Jack cheese** in the butterfly incision on one of the swimps' back and wrap him in a piece of nearly cooked bacon and then throw him on the grill until he turns pink (often pronounced "pank") and the bacon finishes cooking. Right before you take him off the grill, paint him with a big glob of your favorite **sweet, hot barbecue sauce** and then put him on a plate until he cools off enough that the hot cheese won't take the hide off your tongue, and then eat his little ass up!

Fatten-You-Right-Up Rolls

Tammy Donna just insists that we have these little rolls that her mama makes for her all the time. She nearly drowned in her own saliva just telling me how to make 'em on the telephone. I think you'll agree they are pretty fine and very easy, which is even better. All in the world you have to do is mix together **1 stick melted butter, 1 cup sour cream,** and **1 heaping cup self-rising flour**—that is *it*. Put little globs in a greased mini-muffin pan and bake 'em at 400 for about 12 minutes, and there you have it, little bite-sized balls of warm, fluffy fat—a true Southern delicacy.

Of course, the best job in the whole world is not even available to us—not to any of us, not even Oprah or Hillary Clinton. Not even in the Bitch Bar. It's a Queen job, naturally, and (dare I say it?) it's even better than being the Boss of All the Sweet Potato Queens (which job also cannot be held by Oprah or Hillary Clinton, but that's beside the point). Whatever, you ask, could *this* be? Good question. It's the Queen *Bee* job. As such, you would be waited on hand and foot—you would have no hands, of course, but a buttload of feet. Everything you could ever want would be delivered to you by strapping young guy bees. You'd be the only girl in the whole town who gets to have sex, and you get to have it with absolutely everybody, and, in fact, you outlive everybody. Oh, it's quite the gig to have, all right. I don't think we (humans) have anything that measures up, but we're still on the case!

PART II

Fambly Stuff

Daddy the Feeder

When my father died, everybody who came to the funeral called to mind a different food "we would never have again in this life." As you may imagine, this brought on great weeping, wailing, and gnashing of teeth. Daddy was a Feeder. He was driven, compelled by some unseen force, to feed anyone and everyone who crossed his path. He loved to cook, always whistled in the kitchen, and could not be broken of wiping his hands on the seat of his pants. (I share these traits with him and wish more every day that he was here to share that fact with, but I digress.)

Upon entering his house, one could expect to be offered food, starting with whatever it was he happened to be cooking at the moment. If this offer was declined, he would proceed to name off pretty much everything in the refrigerator, freezer, and pantry. This was an exhaustive process. Family and regular visitors had long since learned to give up and just eat something—if for no other reason than it made the man so happy. Of course, once you ate "a little something," your next problem was "how 'bout a little *more?*" We're all fat and have a lot of fat friends as a result. I'm sure he was singlehandedly responsible for a goodly portion of the extraordinarily high percentage of morbid obesity in our home state of Mississippi, certainly in Hinds County.

The man woke me up every day of my life as long as I lived under his roof, asked what I wanted for breakfast, and then trotted off to make it for me—only one of the many reasons I lived under his roof until I was pretty well past grown. Another reason is that he was the funniest human being who ever drew breath. Hardly a day goes by that I don't recount something hilarious Daddy said or did, and he's been dead more than twenty years now. Okay, just for instance, when he was a kid and took chemistry for the first time, he learned how to make a concoction that apparently had sulfuric acid in it, because it stunk to high heaven. He managed to ferret some of it out of the classroom and took it home. "Home" was a frame house, out in the country, heated only by the fireplaces in each room. So much time was spent in the evenings in close quarters, gathered by the roaring fire in the main room of the house. Everybody would be in there, including a number of cats and hound dogs, all minding their tails in a roomful of rocking chairs. Daddy would surreptitiously release the cap on his vial of stinky stuff just long enough for a small cloud of it to waft through the room, enhanced by the heat of the fire. His father, the ineffable Harvey, would glance around and ask the Mother of the house, his wife, Carrie, if one of the kids was in need of a purgative. (This was the popular remedy of that day for *anything* from a headache to a hangnail to a bad attitude—whatever was ailing you, you got some kind of laxative as the first line of defense.) She allowed as how she thought everybody was perking along pretty good. Daddy would bide his time for a bit, and by and by, he'd sneak another leak of the mephitic mess. By this time, Harvey was eyeing the dogs with suspicion. After yet another whiff of the odiferous gas, Harvey sprang to his feet, flung open the doors, and ran all the dogs out into the cold, cussin' 'em for stinking up the house the whole time. At this point, Daddy could contain himself no longer and, weeping with laughter at his own cleverness, he revealed to Harvey the true source of the stench. Whereupon Harvey, completely nonplussed, turned to his helpmeet, Carrie, and said, in sorrowful tones, "I work my fingers to the *bone* to send this boy to school so he can have a better life someday, and *what* do they teach him? How to put a *poot* in a *bottle!*"

Crawfish Étouffée

One of my treasures is a recipe for Crawfish Étouffée, written in Daddy's own handwriting. He got the recipe from his much-beloved Huval buddies in South Louisiana. Daddy loved their cooking, and his favorite part of any coonass recipe was that they all pretty much start the same way: First you make a roux (pronounced "roo" for anybody who doesn't know). To make the roux for this, you put **10 tablespoons oil** in an iron skillet on low heat and stir in **5 tablespoons flour.** Stir that a bunch and cook it until it gets brown—and it takes a while, lemme tell you. While your roux is cooking, put **5 tablespoons oil** in a heavy 4-quart kettle, turn the heat on low, and put in **3 medium onions,** diced and **2 medium bell peppers,** diced, and cook those, stirring often, until the onions are transparent. Then add **8 cups peeled crawfish tails** (Daddy said if crawfish are not available, it's almost as good with shrimp) and **2 quarts water.** Take **1 pint water** and mix it quickly into your roux and then put the roux into the crawfish mixture and cook it over low heat for about 2½ hours until it's thick. Serve it over rice (with a bottle of Crystal Hot Sauce on the side) with a green salad and French bread.

Daddy had written a note at the bottom of the recipe: *Recipe never fails if you love the people for whom it is prepared.*

FINANCIAL TIP

My very first Financial Plan in Life was that Daddy would live forever. If you have a similar plan in place, here's my word of caution: He won't. It is a total bitch, but it's a fact. My advice is to figure out how to take care of yourself while he *is* still alive, even though you don't really have to do it and you know it on account of he carries you around on a little satin pillow and does every thing in the world for you. Knowing how to do it your ownself will come in *so* handy when That Day comes.

8

Sister Judy and Trevor's Louisiana Specialties

I come from a long line of fat, happy people. This automatically tells you that eating is one of our favorite forms of entertainment. It would not be overstatement to say that it's our *only* form of entertainment, but actually it's more like the center of our universe or even the reason for it. The one thing we all agree on: We should eat and we should eat a lot. Eating is the main subject of thought and source of conversation in my family. What shall we eat? When? Who shall prepare which dishes? It is our only form of consolation in times of grief and pain, our drug of choice, if you will. We would never get drunk to get over something; we would eat a pie or a pig or both. It is our chosen field of continuing education and the focus of just about any goal-setting. If something tastes good, we will go to the ends of the earth to get more of it one way or another, even if it requires learning how to make it our ownselves. As my sister, Judy, and I like to say, "Say it loud: We're fat and proud."

Witness the inordinate amount of trouble that our own Trevor Palmer (son of sister Judy and owner of the world-famous F&M Patio Bar in New Orleans) went to in order to get some really good jambalaya. Garden-variety jambalaya is on every corner in the state of Louisiana, but *exceptional* jambalaya is not that easily come by, as you will see. Trevor explains:

"I learned the secret techniques of huge cast-iron sugar-kettle cooking from a true Louisiana master, Blair 'Cockadoo' Lamendola, who is a three- or four-time jamb champ. Every year in Gonzales, Louisiana, they have the Jambalaya Fest, where there is serious competition. You must follow the rules—simple but very tricky: The only ingredients anybody can use are whole chickens, onions, rice, water, salt, and pepper. And you gotta cook it in a big pot—at least thirty gallons—over a wood fire. When I heard about Blair twelve years ago, I grabbed my master crawfish boiler, Joe Cosgrove, and we set out to Gonzales to find him.

"Blair welcomed us right into the back of his store, the guts of his jamb-cooking empire. He had ice-cold canned beer and all the jamb wisdom you could imagine. He also had four hundred-gallon cast-iron kettles going. These are the ones you see in front of old plantation mansions—sometimes they make them into fountains. Each one of these babies had three or four guys with stainless-steel oars working the mixture over burners that could cook a mule. We told him about F&M and how we have lots of private parties and wanted to learn to cook this stuff out on the patio with the guests. He sized us up right away: 'You need a fifty-gallon kettle to start with,' he said, 'plus the oar, lid, stand, burner, and about eight beers apiece.' We accepted his advice and he then let us watch him cook a batch from scratch.

"While the lesson was progressing, Blair's friend Floyd the jeweler, from across the street, came by to visit. Floyd was also the official pot curer. You know the deal with cast-iron frying pans? Rub it with oil and stick it in the oven for a while? Well, *these* pots don't fit in the oven. So Floyd takes over. For a reasonable price, he takes your pot, fills it full of oil, and sticks the whole thing in a wood fire and burns it. He says it cooks off the nasty mess the foundry people put on the kettle. When you get it back, you're ready to go, and he even gives you a picture of your pot, on fire, in his fire. Cosgrove lost my picture, but I still have the pot."

Trevor has strong feelings about two things concerning jambalaya—the taste of it and the kind of pot it's cooked in—and his feelings about both are rooted in his childhood:

"Like most folks in Louisiana, I grew up having the dish at home. My mom made it in the biggest pot we had—a large aluminum stockpot—and she served it in a big iceberg lettuce leaf—you got a plate, too. Her jambalaya doesn't have tomato paste in it, and back then, every restaurant and most New Orleans folks put it in their jamb. I think it makes it taste bitter and it also does strange things to the rice. If you're using paste now, just take it out from now on—you'll be loved by all."

In high school, when Trevor was a legislative page in Baton Rouge, he went to a Cajun party where they had huge black cast-iron pots filled with jambalaya. He never forgot it.

"The rice was dark brown and tasted even better than Mom's. My grandfather—we called him PawPaw—had the same kind of pot these good ole boys used for their jamb. PawPaw used it to boil peanuts for us up in Jackson every summer. He built up a wood fire in the yard, set the pot on, and we played all afternoon in the swimming pool until the peanuts were done. Soft and salty—with an Old Milwaukee, once I was old enough—it was the real deal."

Trevor's PawPaw was, of course, my daddy, and the pot he had was his mama's wash pot; she would fill it with water, soap, and dirty clothes and build a fire around it, and that was how the clothes got washed pre-Maytag. I have fond memories of Daddy and that pot, too. Those boiled peanuts were legendary, and I would eat them until my lips were like corrugated paper from the salt. Sometimes Daddy would go out somewhere in the country early, early in the morning to a place where you could pick your own corn, and he'd pick a car-trunkful of the sweetest white corn in the world and bring it home and boil it for us in that pot. After we ate all we could hold of the corn, he'd bring out the ice-cold watermelons. It pleases me that Trevor now has that old black pot and that he's still cooking good stuff in it for people he loves.

Trevor's Famous F&M Patio Jambalaya

Brown **2 pounds good hot sausage** and **1 pound ham** (not processed ham) in a heavy-bottomed pot, then add **1 pound chicken meat,** cut up (white, dark, whatever you like) and brown that, too. Add 5 **chopped onions, 4 ribs chopped celery, 2 chopped bell peppers,** and a **beer.** Stir and make sure nothing is sticking to the bottom of the pot. Cook until the onions are clear and then add **1 20-ounce can whole tomatoes** (kinda mash 'em and tear 'em up with your hands) and cook for 10 minutes. Add **7 cups chicken stock, 5 bay leaves, 1 tablespoon basil, 1 tablespoon thyme, 1 tablespoon chili powder,** and **salt and pepper to taste,** and simmer it all for 20 minutes. Stir in **4 cups real rice** (not converted) and bring it to a high boil for 4 minutes, then cover and reduce the heat to the absolute lowest it will go. *Don't lift the lid off the pot for 20 minutes.* Then check the rice. Turn it from bottom to top—don't stir or whip it like mashed potatoes. Taste the rice—if it needs more time, cover and cook for another 10 minutes.

I've eaten Trevor's jambalaya and it is the best I've ever had, so if you want to make it, do like he says. He is particularly adamant about us not lifting the lid off for those 20 minutes. He swears it will be inedible if we do that. Of course, that makes me wild to take the lid off—just to see what will happen—but I'm not willing to risk him actually being right and me screwing up a whole big giant pot of jambalaya, so I mind him. You should, too.

My sister, Judy, moving off to New Orleans a number of years ago (about forty or so) has certainly added to our Fun and Food Repertoires. All through my teenage years my buddies and I would pile in on Judy for Mardi Gras and Jazz Fest—or to hear all the hottest live-music acts in the country play at the various bars she and her husband, the infamous Jed, owned—and to do a little dranking. Back then, you could drink at eighteen in Louisiana, and we took advantage of that fact, not that anybody in New Orleans has ever cared how old anybody is—if you've got the money and can reach the counter, you can order a drink. Parents had keg parties for their junior-high-school kids just to beat the rush for budding alcoholism, for which most kids have to wait until their freshman year in college—very progressive.

At any rate, on the way to New Orleans from Jackson, Mississippi, down I-55, you pass—but not ever without stopping—a place called Pass Manchac, which is home to a restaurant called Middendorf's, where they serve something called "thin fish." I'm telling you, no matter where you live in the USA, it would be worth the trouble for you to get in your car right this minute and head to Middendorf's for the sole purpose of getting some thin fish. What it is is just the thinnest, lightest, most delectable catfish on the planet. It's fried, naturally, and irresistibly yummy. So to this day, whenever we go to New

Orleans to visit Judy, we stop—coming and going—at Midden-dorf's for an order of thin fish and a Dixie beer.

FINANCIAL TIP

Get the *large* order of thin fish.

An added attraction at Middendorf's has always been the ladies' room—just to see people try to figure it out. This has always been in the Top Ten Weirdest bathrooms I've ever been in. For years it was just your basic yellowy-painted wood, but it was a long, narrow, corridor-type affair. Clearly a man had designed it because the stall doors were about ten inches away from the toilets. This means that, even if you were the tiniest woman in the world, you could not actually sit on the potty and close the door at the same time. If someone walked by your stall, they would see the door standing slightly ajar and try to close it for you, whacking you in the knees or completely dislodging you from your perch; if you were performing the time-honored midair hover, you were set in motion. You'd see people, obviously in there for the first time, going in and out of every stall, trying to find one that fit or to figure out what *they* were doing wrong.

Then, one day, we went in expecting the same room and whoa! were *we* ever surprised. They had put all the stalls at the end of the corridor, but the doors were the same and you still couldn't sit and close the doors at the same time, so we knew we were still at Middendorf's. It remained that way for a number of years, so imagine our surprise when we ventured in there after a thoroughly satisfying feast of thin fish and discovered the whole room had been transformed from a commonplace, poorly designed *pissoir* into a romantically lit meat locker. You can actually now go in a stall, sit down, and close the door. The bizarre part is the walls: The lower half is brushed stainless steel, the upper half expensively swathed in a very dark wallpaper. The ceiling is black with black track-light canisters. It looks like the inside of a spaceship or at least the restroom of a spaceship. It is so weird—especially when you're coming from the rest of the restaurant, which still has the same old wood paneling and cypress knees and linoleum. This rest room is like some kind of mutant tumor growing off the side of the restaurant's head. But it's fun to stumble on something totally incongruous and outlandish every now and then—yanks one out of complacency.

But anyway, Judy has learned to cook all manner of wonderful dishes that we wouldn't normally have had on our tables in Mississippi. One of my favorite New Orleans foods is Crawfish Monica. Michael Rubenstein used to spoon-feed it to me at Jazz Fest every year. Don't you find that having a handsome man with winning ways, a lot of money, and a hard-on for you spoon-feeding you delicious food that he paid for just enhances the whole experience? I know I do. But Judy taught me how to make the Monica my ownself, in case Rube should wander off sometime. How fortuitous.

Judy's Crawfish Monica

It's real easy, but it doesn't taste like it. First, cook 1¹/₂ **pounds of rotini pasta** (don't overcook it, for goodness' sake—learn what *al dente* means) and set it aside to cool off. All you do then is heat **2 sticks sweet butter** in a deep skillet until it's bubbly hot and then stir in **3 tablespoons Cajun seasoning,** blending it well. Then you pour in 1¹/₂ **quarts heavy cream** and cook it down until it's reduced by half. Throw in **1 cup green onions,** chopped, the cooled-off pasta, and 1¹/₂ **pounds of crawfish tail meat,** and cook it just till everything gets hot—it doesn't take a whole lot of time to cook the crawfish.

Get a handsome man with winning ways and a hard-on for you to spoon-feed it to you and tell *me* Crawfish Monica isn't the best thing you ever ate.

FINANCIAL TIP

Money isn't everything.

9

Mother Moves In

My mother has been living with me and my daughter, BoPeep, for a number of years. For those of you who've not yet crossed over into the eerie realm of becoming a parent to your parents, I offer the perspective provided by my journal of the events in our lives that led to Mother Moving In.

December 10, 1996: I must have done something really hideous in a previous life—judging from the kind of week I've just been through. It had to have been in a prior lifetime because I have never been indicted in this one, and if I had committed any crime deserving of all this, I should be in, like, lifetime solitary confinement, eating moldy bread and drinking stagnant water, breaking rocks in the hot sun, etc. I cannot imagine what I could have done to warrant this kind of week—but believe me, whatever it is, I am sorry for it. I do most heartily repent of it whatever it was—just dee-liver me from another week like it.

Last week: I had pneumonia. And a bladder infection. Spent two hours at the Doc-in-the-Box. Spent forty-five minutes in line waiting for prescriptions—with both illnesses worsening by the nanosecond. Had adverse reaction to medications. Spent hours tracking down the Doc-in-the-Box doc to get new drugs. Another forty-five minutes in line at the drugstore. My car blew up and BoPeep got out of school for the Christmas holidays—ready to be entertained. And last, my mother had a stroke!

Some may think it self-absorbed of me to list my mother's stroke in a compilation of Really Inconvenient Things That Happened to Me. Obviously their mothers don't do for them what my mother does for me. My mother being out of commission is like a postal strike, transit strike, garbage strike, air-traffic controllers' strike, firefighters', cops', and teachers' strike, and a computer meltdown all rolled into one.

It's like everything that's good and wonderful and pleasant in life has shut down and the only things left in operation are dentists, telemarketers, and the IRS. Lots of pills to swallow and no water. Big plates of cornbread, no milk. Flat tire in the middle of the Delta in August and no spare. Total-body cast, itchy nose. Trouble with a really big T.

My mother, like, makes life possible. *I cannot begin to list all the stuff she does for me in a day. Stuff that there is not enough money in the* world *to pay somebody to do for me. My mother not only does Big Stuff that needs doing—she will Run Errands for me.*

Running Errands is my most *unfavorite thing in the whole world to do. She's not wild about it, either, but she does it for me—all day long. It's a Mom Thing. I'm talking—the woman comes to my house at 4:45—*A.M.—*three days a week so I can work. [I was doing personal fitness training for clients at the time.] She does my last night's dishes, folds any laundry, irons 'Peep's uniform, serves 'Peep breakfast in bed, makes 'Peep's lunch, and gets her ready for school. Try to think of any person who would do that for you—or any person for whom* you *would do it. It's a Major Mom Thing.*

Thankfully, the prognosis is very good. The doctors tell us she will be slightly disoriented for the next couple of weeks and then she should be fine with some medication. The main effect we're seeing right now is a case of hyper-cheerfulness and mild goofiness. Apparently the stroke has seized on some qualities she already possessed and heightened them somewhat.

Mother Moves In

She's always fairly cheerful and just the tiniest bit off. Not dumb, not by a long shot—no, what I'm talking about is she's always been on a slightly different track. You're never qui-i-i-i-te sure what she's going to say. Add to that the fact that she usually means something entirely different from what she actually says. My sister, Judy, and I have spent our lives on tenterhooks whenever she's around our friends. Mother is perfectly capable of the "You don't sweat much for a fat girl"–type comment. She really means to say something nice, not a mean bone in her body, but somehow it will come out askew and Judy and I are just on the floor.

You have to understand, in my family, we deal with everything by laughing at it. So what I'm saying is, this stroke thing has not been totally bereft of humor. Mother called me on a Saturday afternoon to tell me she was "sleepy—so very sleepy." I'm going, Hey, thanks for the update, Mom, go take a nap. She was supposed to go to a Christmas party and she was too sleepy, she said. She had plenty of time for a nap, so I told her to go take one, and I'd call her back in an hour and wake her up. Of course, when I called her back, she couldn't wake up right and she was slurring her words and I knew what had happened. I went and sacked her up and took her to the ER. But through it all, she's been cognizant of everything, with her usual cockeyed reactions to it all. For instance, she knew she was slurring her words and couldn't keep her eyes open, but her thoughts were: "How am I gonna talk at this party?" Not "Holy shit! I could be dying here!" But rather, "How will I ever dominate the conversation when I can't even form consonants?"

The slurring has all gone now. It has been replaced by this totally new voice that sounds like Aunt Bea (from the old Andy Griffith shows)—on a real happy day. You call her hospital room and she answers, about four octaves higher than she's ever spoken before, "Hello-o-o-o!"

While I was out of her room, she told everyone who called that she was going home and they should come over and drink coffee. I spent the afternoon and evening undoing that. There were twenty people sitting coffeeless in her driveway before I figured out what she had done. I drove the nurses crazy because she was so unwavering in her belief that she was, in fact, going home, that I would start to believe it and have to call to verify.

The doctors tell us she will be "normal" in a couple of weeks. We sincerely hope not. If she was normal, she wouldn't have anything to do with us!

And did I mention that during her unfortunate confinement, I have been wearing her jewelry?

Mother got out of the hospital and returned to her own home and everything was fine for some months until . . . (You always know to expect the very worst anytime you read something was "fine until." This time is no different.)

I came home one day and received a weirder-than-usual message from her on my voice mail. All she said was, "I feel so funny—I just hate this for you, baby," and the phone went dead. When I called her back and got no answer, I just flung BoPeep in the car and headed across town. 'Peep was round-eyed and scared: "Is she dead, Mama?" I said I didn't know yet, but yes, she might be, but it would be okay, no matter what—if she's dead, she's already in heaven and there's nothing for us to worry about, but let's just go see about her. I called to have an ambulance meet me there, fully expecting the worst. It was not great but not nearly the worst. She had fallen—and she couldn't speak. I initially thought she'd had another stroke, but it turned out she had bitten her tongue when she fell, and with the big wad of Coumadin she takes every day, her poor tongue had swelled up and turned as black as a chow dog's and she just couldn't make it work for her.

After another round of hospital care, the medical professionals still had no idea what had happened to her and she was released once again and allowed to go home. A few *more* months went by, uneventfully—and yeah, there's another "until" here. This time she was at church and she just casually mentioned, thank God, to one of her church buddies, that she "felt funny—just like before," and boy, they had an ambulance there in the biggest jiffy they could muster up. I met them at the ER, and just as they were preparing to take her off for a CT scan, she had the biggest seizure I've ever personally witnessed. It's a terrifying thing, but certainly the conditions for it were perfect—every doctor on duty was in there with her. This was also good because it provided the much-needed information we were looking for—namely, what the hell was going on with her. We now knew she was having seizures as a result of the stroke. Treatable. Good. *However,* she would not be allowed to *drive* until she had been seizure-free for six months—which meant she was Moving In with Me.

The good news is, it was not another stroke and there is no apparent damage—to her, anyway. I, personally, am getting a little frayed around the edges. Who, I would just like to know, is supposed to run my errands if they won't let my mama drive? No one cares about that! All I can say is there's either gonna be a boom time for cabs around here or there's just a whole passel of stuff that ain't gonna get done.

I guess I'll just sack her up and move her in with me when they let her out of the hospital. I told her she can't be over there having fits by herself, she's likely to hurt herself and break a bunch of stuff besides. And furthermore, I told her, if I am going to have to find you dead, I'd just as soon you be in the next room—no point in me having to fight five o'clock traffic all the way across town, wondering what I was gonna find when I got there.

Mother Moves In

*   *   *

But this is gonna be great. I will get to be the Boss of Everything. Remember growing up, the arbitrary rules they had that didn't make any sense then, and now that you're grown up, they still don't? It seemed like a gratuitous exercise of authority to me. My own personal mother had this thing about how much bathwater everybody ought to use. I have no earthly idea what it was about. It was way before conservation was even invented—and water was just dirt cheap, y'know? It couldn't have been the money. For whatever reason, she, herself, did not like to take long baths in neck-deep hot water, and so it became a Rule That Nobody Else Could, Either. Whenever she was gone, I would take just such baths—often one right after the other, just for spite. By now I have practically elevated bathing to "hobby" status—and the pleasure of it is always enhanced by the sure knowledge that it would drive her crazy if she knew.

Well, if she's gonna be living here, she's gonna have to play by the rules. Yes, indeedy-do, she will, and the Number One Rule will be: All bath water must be not only very deep but very hot as well, and no bath will take less than 45 minutes.

Strokes are peculiar things—there are so many different aftereffects to choose from. We have no paralysis, thank God, or any of the other easily recognizable sequelae. We got this sort of hit-or-miss Weirdness. We— and by "we," I mean She, Mother, Herself, naturally—go along, looking and acting as normal as possible for any-body in this family, and then just out of nowhere, It strikes. It will take root over some insignificant event; nobody suspects that anything out of the ordinary is happening. But unbeknownst to the rest of the family—which consists of me and BoPeep—Mother is off some-where obsessing about the Insignificant Thing and working herself into a froth over it. Once it reaches crit-ical mass, anything can happen and often does.

For instance: Last week, 'Peep was out carousing with her father, the erstwhile MoonPie, Mother had been doing quite well, and so I told Mother that Tammy and I were thinking of running down to Hal and Mal's to see the Iguanas perform later that night. I called Hal and Mal's and learned that the Iguanas would not be going on until eleven-thirty—for me that is practically the next morning. But I was determined, so I took a nap, just so I could stay up long enough to go out. So when eleven-thirty rolled around, I tiptoed out the front door and headed downtown—without Tammy, who pulled up lame on me at the last minute. The Iguanas played for exactly one hour, including exactly one encore, and I was back home, in bed and sound asleep, by 12:45.

I am just snoozing away, completely oblivious to the Tempest that was brewing across the hall. Four A.M.—I am still snoozing away, blissfully unaware, but not for long because about 4:03 A.M., the mother across the hall managed to switch on every light in the house and open

*and close at least six doors—all simultaneously—and
one of those doors and one of those lights were in my own
personal room. And all the while she was demanding to
know, Was I in there?* Color *me pleased. I advised her,
as pleasantly as possible, all things considered, that, yes,
I was in there and that I had been in there for at least
four hours and until just very recently had been sound
asleep for the entire four hours and what in the world
was she doing up and what possible difference could
it make if I was in there or not? Did she need me for
something? Was she sick?* Thirsty? What? *What is it?
What do you want? She didn't know. All she knew was
she had awakened two hours earlier and she didn't hear
me come in and she'd been just lying there for two hours
worrying about where I was, etc.*

*The next day, I asked her, What in the world were
you thinking? What were you going to do if I wasn't
there? If I am dead somewhere, you'll find out soon
enough—no need to go looking around in the middle of
the night. No news is good news and all that. I am an old
woman myself—I'll come home when I'm ready—
which, by the way, is hardly ever after dark anymore. The
Weirdness Factor is that she never* did *have any idea as
to why it was so all-fired important for her to determine
if I was in there or not. All she knew was that at the time
it was very important. So naturally, now, I spend every
night with some small part of my brain awake—waiting
for Bed Check. Ahhh, yes, life in the Old Folks' Home.*

*   *   *

Mother is no longer among the Cooking (though still very much among the Eating), but when she did cook, she could make some mighty fine desserts. Here are three of them.

Lemon Yumbo

Mix 1¼ cup coconut, ¾ cup fine saltine cracker crumbs, ½ cup sugar, ½ cup flour and 1 stick butter, soft or melted. This is your crust—you're seeing the Yumbo part already, yes? Put half of it in an 8-by-8-inch pan. Now mix ½ cup sugar, 2½ tablespoons cornstarch, and ¼ teaspoon salt, then add 1⅓ cup milk to it and cook it over low heat until it gets thick, stirring it the whole time. Mix 1 beaten egg with ¼ teaspoon lemon juice and add a little bit of the hot milk mixture to it and then add the warm lemon/egg stuff to the rest of the hot milk stuff and cook and stir all that over low heat for 2 minutes. Add ½ teaspoon grated lemon peel, 1 tablespoon butter, and a few drops of vanilla.

Mix that all up and pour it into the coconut crust, then put the remaining half of the crust stuff on top and bake it at 400 for about 25 minutes or just until it turns golden brown on the top. Then you chill it in the fridge for a while—this is the hardest part, not eating it immediately: It's got that sweet/salty combo thing going, *plus* the lemony thing. I usually just go on and double the recipe from the beginning—one little ole pan is not ever gonna be enough, especially if somebody else wants a bite.

Gooiest Cake in the World

Another of Mother's specialties was this yummy cake. You start with **1 yellow cake mix** (not the pudding kind), mixed up with **3 eggs, ¹/₄ cup water, 1 teaspoon baking soda, ¹/₄ teaspoon salt,** and **1 20-ounce can crushed pineapple.** Bake it however the cake mix says to and then ice it with this: Melt together **2 sticks butter** and mix it with **1 cup evaporated milk** and **1¹/₂ cups sugar,** then add **1 small can (7-ounce) Angel Flake Coconut.** Poke holes in the cake and pour this stuff over it. As soon as it cools off just the slightest bit, put your face in it.

Mystery Slush

Okay, this stuff is weird yet wonderful, but you cannot tell *anybody* what's in it because it has dates in it. Now, me, I think dates are great, but a lot of people are funny about them for some unknown reason. I fed this stuff to one girl, who was eating it like a big ole *hawg* until I told her it had dates in it, whereupon she made a face and said, "You shouldn't have told me that—I hate dates," and she seriously wouldn't eat another bite. Now, I ask you, is this the obnoxious behavior of a four-year-old or what? She was probably forty at the time—doesn't it make you want to smack her? Besides being just plain ole garden-variety *rude*, it was also totally without logic and reason, since she'd already enthusiastically eaten probably a pound of the stuff. Oh, well, I happily finished her leavings as well as the rest of the batch.

Mash up a bunch of **Oreos (at least 16)** to make the crust. Smoosh it into a pie plate and then eat the rest of the bag of Oreos while you're cooking the filling, which goes like this: Bring to a boil **8 ounces of chopped dates**, **¹/₂ teaspoon salt**, and **1 cup water**, then reduce the heat and simmer it for 3 minutes. Remove it from the heat and add **2 cups miniature marshmallows**. Let that cool off some and add **1 running-over teaspoon vanilla** and **¹/₂ cup chopped pecans**. Blend all this together and pour it into the Oreo crust. Whip **¹/₂ pint whipping cream** and put it on top, sprinkle some Oreo crumbs over the top (if you left any anywhere), and throw on some pecan halves. Chill and serve, but remember, mum's the word—unless, of course, you want to eat it all yourself, in which case, blab away.

FINANCIAL TIP

If there's any moving in with grown children/relatives to be done, try to be the one doing the moving in. My mother has the best deal in the universe. I used to think the creatures with the easiest, most pampered lives in the world were my various dogs and cats. They sleep all day and night, people pet them and hand-feed them round the clock, they are responsibility-free. But Mother's even got them beat. She can drive a car and she's got her own room and a credit card!

I tell BoPeep on a semiregular basis that I'm taking notes on Mother's gig here, because I'll be moving in with *her* as soon as she graduates from college—high school if she can afford her own apartment then. By all means, live with your children as soon as possible. Sit down in the middle of the road and declare yourself Helpless. It looks like a great life to me. Those who have to wait on you night and day may yammer and complain from time to time, but you don't hear so good, either—remember?

ALTERNATE PLAN

As soon as possible after college, become the child who lives far, far away.

I will say having Mother living with me has given me a whole new slant on the aging thing, and it's also given me a warped sense of hope. Now, Mama was always a Large Woman—tall and also big—and she was always battling the pounds. But for some reason, for the last five or six years, she's just been getting smaller and smaller. She's shorter—a lot shorter—and she's also about four sizes smaller, and it's just a big mystery because you have never seen the likes of the crap this woman eats. When I'm in town, I cook supper every night, always pretty healthy stuff, but all day long and when I'm out of town, she eats pure-dee crap—frozen stuff with no nutritional value whatsoever that I can discern. I read the label on one thing and I swear to you it had over 650 calories in a serving and 50-plus grams of fat— with no fiber. Lard is not *that* fattening. What could they possibly be doing to this stuff to get so much fat in it? And she just laps it up. I can leave the refrigerators and freezers (we have multiples of both) full of already-cooked healthy stuff and she will absolutely leave it in there till it rots in favor of the crap. And she gets smaller every day! I don't know if it's because of one of her four thousand daily medications or if it has something to do with her stroke or *what*, but whatever it is—I want some of it.

She eats an entire pie by herself every other day. Let me try to communicate to you just how annoying it is, not only that she eats four pies a week by herself, but that I am the one who is forced to go to the grocery store in inclement weather to procure her pies. Heaven help us if we run out of pies around here! And she guards those pies, too, let me tell you. If anybody else eats some of one, she knows it and comments, in tones of shock and disdain, on just how much of it they ate. But it's hard to tell if she thinks the person ate too large a portion to be healthy or comfortable (talk about your pot talking bad about the kettle!) or if she's just pissed they ate some of *her* precious pie. In any event, you come away knowing that she considers any and all pie products to be her personal domain and that it would probably be best for all if you just got your own damn pie.

I feel oddly hopeful about all this for myself and my friends. Some of us have daughters, and we cannot wait to get old, move in with them, and start making them fetch us pies, which we will sit and eat out of the pan with our hands. We can't wait to eat crap and get skinny. We may take up smoking, too. And sky-diving. Anything dangerous or unhealthy. On our seventy-fifth birthdays, we're gonna commence doing it all, and we're gonna make our children drive us around and fetch our cigarettes and pies for us. What's that about wearing purple when we get old? *Ha!* We intend to get more dangerous with each and every passing year.

I was entirely carried away with recent news articles about plastic surgery in the elderly being up by 364 percent! I read about one woman who had just had the works—breast implants, face-lift, eyes done. Everything that could be hiked up *was*, and she was eighty years old! I hope that when I'm eighty I still care enough about having tits to get some new ones. Doesn't that just perk you up? I hope she lives another fifty years and gets a lot of mileage out of her new stuff.

Drop~Dead~Easy Pots de Crème

In the rare emergency situation when we have somehow inadvertently run out of pies, a quick—very quick—recipe is needed so Mother may have her "fix" and I don't have to leave the house in the pouring rain to fetch a pie. Damon Lee Fowler, the author of *Damon Lee Fowler's New Southern Kitchen* (Simon & Schuster), one of your more excellent cookbooks, sent me the Very Thing—and it's chocolate! He calls this Drop-Dead-Easy Pots de Crème, and it is so easy, you don't even have to cook it. It would seem that Damon Lee has met us before and knows just how slackass lazy we really are.

Here's all you have to do: Heat ³/₄ **cup cream** just to the boiling point. Put **1 egg, 6 ounces semisweet chocolate bits** (also known as chocolate chips), ¹/₈ **teaspoon salt,** and **2 tablespoons sugar** in a blender and blend it for about 20 seconds at high speed. (Twenty seconds is just the right amount of time to spend in the kitchen, isn't it?) Take the little cover out of the center hole in the blender lid and, while the blender's still running, gradually pour the hot cream in. Turn the machine off and scrape the stuff off the sides of the blender, then add **1 table-spoon bourbon** or **brandy** and give it another whirl, just for a few seconds to mix it in. And, hey, you are done! Now all you do is pour the stuff into lidded pots-de-crème pots or demitasse cups and chill. That is according to Damon Lee, who is concerned with presentation and all that. Me, I just pour it all into a bowl for *one* and sit Mother down right by the refrigerator with her spoon to wait for the stuff to cool off enough to eat.

Atlanta Allelujah!

Karen Spector, a favored member of the Worldwide Sweet Potato Queen Movement, Pie Kappa Yamma, came out to see me on my Atlanta stop when I was touring for *God Save the Sweet Potato Queens*, and, sweet thing that she is, she brought me this wonderful cake—right when I needed a "little something" most of all. Saved me from a major swooning, sinking spell is all she did. Therefore, I call it Atlanta Allelujah! When the situation is not quite the Def-Con 5 Emergency and we've got a little time, sometimes I make this for Mother and it makes her pretty happy, too.

All you need is **1 chocolate cake mix,** which you mix up with **1 egg** and **1 stick melted butter.** You put that in a lightly greased 9-by-13-inch pan and then you mix up this other stuff: **1 8-ounce package softened cream cheese, 2 eggs, 1 teaspoon vanilla, 1 stick melted butter** (lots of butter in this, yum!), and **³/₄ cup peanut butter.** After that's mixed up pretty good, you add

1 16-ounce box of powdered sugar and mix all that up good. Then you spread it all over the cake stuff in the pan and bake it at 350 for about 40 to 50 minutes—but watch it, you want the center to be a little gooey, so don't overcook it. It smells so good when it's cooking, however, that I think you'll be in greater danger of scalding yourself trying to eat it while it's still *in* the oven than you'll ever be of overcooking it.

It's a Miracle! Pie

Imagine a dark and stormy night—a pieless Mother is standing before the pieless refrigerator, looking at me in a meaningful way, telling me in that wordless yet eloquent way of hers that "only pie will suffice, so don't bother with any other offerings." I am not much for venturing out on dark and stormy nights, but neither am I just sitting around waiting to make somebody a pie. This recipe is for just such occasions.

Get your blender out and dump in **1 cup sugar, 4 eggs, 2 cups milk, $^1\!/_2$ cup melted butter, $^1\!/_2$ cup flour, 1 running-over teaspoon vanilla, 1 cup flaked coconut,** and a **dash salt.** (If your blender is in immediate danger of overflowing, don't panic—just put as much milk in as you can, blend it all, and then add the remaining milk afterward.) Pour all that into a 10-inch pie pan and bake it at 300 until it sets—about an hour. It makes its own crust all by its ownself—it's a miracle! Serves 6 to 8 regular people or one pieless Mother.

PART III

Food
for Big~Ass
Occasions

10

Ah, Motherhood

Talk about your time-consuming project! I remember when BoPeep was a tee-tiny little thing, I thought I'd still be breast-feeding when she started going on car-dates. There were days when it seemed like she was this twenty-pound refrigerator magnet stuck to my chest for about nineteen of the twenty-four hours. I got so sick of Being Lunch. Giant hickies covered my body, since if I was a little slow in producing the much-desired titties at the *instant* that she desired them, she would just attach herself to any exposed flesh—

neck, wrist, knee, whatever—and commence sucking. I swore that as soon as she got any teeth at all, I was gonna put her on a strict diet of Jujubes. Lactation is not amusing. Trust me. But, hey, now that I'm no longer in the business, here's something entertaining to do: Sneak up behind a lactating woman and say, "Wa-a-a-a-a!" and watch her soak the front of her shirt.

I thought that people were incredibly rude to pregnant women, and I was right, but it doesn't end with the delivery. No-o-o indeed. You are then a target for a whole new set of insults and infuriating questions. Before, when you were pregnant and gaining weight on a hourly basis, they would ask, "How much weight have you gained?" with variations on the inflection to communicate the nuances of their true horror at how staggering the number of pounds must actually be. Now that you have this tiny little pea of a baby to show for all that preproduction padding, they don't ask how much weight have you *lost*. No, it's much more hurtful if they phrase it something like, "How much do you *still have to lose?*" And they get an expression on their face that is heavy with the implication that you will never in a million years lose all that weight, not if you stop eating right this minute and turn yourself into a perpetual-motion machine. No, even then you will still be pudgy, if not downright fat.

But if people are rude to the moms, their treatment pales in comparison to what the poor babies endure on an hourly basis. People would walk up to me and BoPeep—I'd be standing there holding this limp, seemingly lifeless blob o'flesh, a baby that was clearly dead-to-the-world asleep—and they'd grab a hunk of her baby belly, pinch her and say, "Hey, fella—can you smile?" I used to wish she could just pop her eyes open and shout, "Hey! Smile at *this*, asshole, can't you see I'm *sleeping* here?" She'd be dressed in so much pink and lace and froufrou, you could hardly tell there was an actual baby in there, and people would look blank and ask, "Is it a boy or a girl?" I told a few of 'em to "meet Mitch—we like to think he's the world's youngest drag queen."

But anyway, I had my own theories on why women would race back to work after giving birth. I always thought they were just pussies. Hell, a guy can get up and go to the office after a quick stop at the Baby Dump—how hard can that be? It takes a Real Woman to hang out with a tiny person who doesn't so much want a bite of your sandwich as just to suck on it for a while. That's the measure of the *real* Working Mother.

And you know what that mom needs: She needs some strong medicine, something so good, she could weep over it, but at the same time, something so easy, it practically cooks itself— she won't even have to stir it. I can't think of anybody who deserves this fabulous food more than a mom, new or otherwise. We could go so far as to say that you must have given birth to even qualify for eating this stuff, but we won't—we'll share it with everybody. (In my opinion, people who've never had children just don't have shit to do. I mean, what do they *do* with all their time? Of course, they're *busy* and all that, but you moms know what I'm talking about. You've still got all that stuff the non-moms have—plus all that mom-stuff. You get to do it *all*— all the time, at the same time.)

Pig Candy

Anyway, Pig Candy is what I had in mind for your little treat. You just can't even imagine how good this is—and how easy, which makes it even better. You start with **bacon**—and don't y'all just know how I purely love a recipe that starts with bacon! I myself like Bryan thick-sliced bacon, but any good bacon will do. Now, that's redundant, isn't it—like there's bad bacon? Well, actually, I guess there is. I really hate that lean bacon—you know, the kind that has less fat, and they act like that's a good thing. The fat is the whole point of bacon. If you're interested in the red part, get a ham or something. I mean, really. Lean bacon, my ass.

So anyway, you start with bacon, and the only other ingredient is **brown sugar**—and do I really need to say the dark brown kind? You just roll the bacon in the dark brown sugar and then you bake it (at 350 for about 20 minutes or so, depending on your oven and also how you like your bacon—put it on a rack on a cookie sheet and you don't even have to turn it over!)— and *voy-ola!* Pig Candy!

Now, the first time I ever tasted this, I was on the book tour for *God Save the Sweet Potato Queens.* I was in Kansas City and I had pneumonia and I had just that afternoon accidentally said "shit" on live radio and I was feeling like it. But then, *then,* I went to Rainy Day Books and met about ten jillion Queens and had a very large time, and one of those wonderful women (Patti Leathers—I tear up just thinking of her) came up and, with a conspiratorial grin, handed me a large paper sack, saying that, in her opinion, the contents constituted a pretty swell "hotel munchie." I smelled bacon without even opening the bag, and I couldn't wait to get back to my hotel room to be alone with it. Later that evening, I called home to report to one of my own Queens, Tammy, that I was ensconced in my giant hotel bed and was completely happy, having single-handedly consumed an *entire* sack of bacon that had been cooked in brown sugar. I thought she was going to crawl through the telephone.

And then, when I was moving to my new house, our precious darling George showed up to help me (read: do it for me), and what do you reckon he had gotten up at six o'clock in the morning to make for me on moving day? Pig Candy, of course. And do you know that he also added **chopped pecans** to the dark brown sugar? Tammy showed up, too; she has some kind of bacon radar or something. The Pig Candy with pecans was so good, I thought we might just ascend directly into heaven, but we didn't, so I still had to pack and move. But Tammy was so cheered by the bacon that even she hung around and helped.

And I'll have you know that our very own chef, Chris Lambert, at our very own Crowne Plaza Hotel in Jackson, Mississippi, makes Pig Candy for the Million Queen Marchers for the Sunday brunch after Mal's St. Paddy's Parade. That is why the CP is the Only Hotel We Ever Really Loved, and Chris is our Official Most Beloved Chef.

Ah, Pig Candy—so good, only a Real Mother deserves it.

FINANCIAL TIP

If you happen to own a business and you need a manager, you want somebody with a lot of experience so that *you* won't have to do the job *for* them or have to hire a couple of assistants to help out. Go find yourself a single mom with a houseful of kids. She can run your company without even thinking about it—what's one more thing to her? Why anybody would hire a married man to run a business is beyond me.

11

Big~Ass Parties for Teeny~Ass Kids

Lord, help me, by the time you read this, my precious baby girl, BoPeep, will likely be driving cars—and, even worse, riding in 'em with boy-type people. *Egad!* (I've never known what the hell *egad* was even supposed to mean, and so I just stopped right in the middle of this and looked it up! One of the many benefits of having a big-ass publisher like Random House is free books, such as dictionaries. And so I whipped out my big-ass dictionary from Random House and looked up *egad*, and whaddya know, there it was in the actual dictionary all the time. I've been going around needlessly ignorant for years. *Egad*, according to my big-ass Random House dictionary, means "Oh, God." It is what's known in dictionary circles as a "softened euphemism." My own personal mama no doubt wishes I was better versed in the art of the "softened euphemism.")

Anyway, it is just completely incomprehensible to me that BoPeep is practically all growed-up, as we are fond of saying down South even though we *do* know better—thank you very much. I am so very glad that I listened to all those people who told me constantly, "You better hold that baby while you can, because you'll turn around once and she'll be all growed-up." And danged, if they weren't right. I still make her let me hold her at least once a day, but now there are big hunks of her hanging off my lap, where she used to fit so compactly. Sigh.

There is one aspect of this growing-up process that holds great appeal for me, however. That would be that we outgrow the need for the Annual Birthday Party. I hate children's birthday parties with a deep and fearful loathing. There is nothing I can think of right offhand that I would not do to avoid attending one, and I would go to even greater lengths to avoid giving one, even for my own precious daughter, who is my entire heart and I would cheerfully die for her in the slowest, most painful way imaginable, if only she will not make me give her a birthday party ever again.

This is no doubt one of the many proofs that could be held up to demonstrate What a Terrible Mother I Am. And not only did I despise giving birthday parties, I was also a complete failure at Soccer-Momdom. I don't care what they're doing, I don't wanna watch 'em! 'Peep ran track one year and I thought I was gonna die. One track meet takes at least five or six hours, at the end of which BoPeep would do something that takes about thirty seconds to complete and I would be positively wild to escape. I hope there will be any number of ways that BoPeep will testify, in word and deed, that I *am* a Good Mother, but suffice it to say, they won't be your usual June Cleaver traits.

But anyway, the kid birthday party deal. It has long been my opinion that the best method we could, as a society, employ to reduce the Teen Birth Rate would be to make them all work at Chuck E. Cheese for the entire summer of their fifteenth year. Right before they get turned loose in cars by themselves, we should give them a big dose of Hideous Small Children—a big dose over a sustained period of time. I bet they wouldn't have sex before they were thirty!

We have utilized a similar technique with Jay Sones, our captive computer nerd. I call him that with the utmost love and adoration. He is the darling eldest son of one of the Queens, Tammy, and he was forced to work on our Web site (www.sweetpotatoqueens.com) for a number of years for no money at all; we just kept him chained to his computer and we nagged him a lot and made him do stuff for us for free. All that's changed now and we pay him huge sums of money, although we have not slacked up noticeably on the nagging. But one of the side benefits of Jay's employment and subsequent heavy involvement with the Worldwide Sweet Potato Queen Movement is that we have personally insured that Jay will not marry prematurely or in a cavalier manner. No, indeed. Our Jay will give the matrimonial issue his absolute Best Thought for a reeeeeeeeeally long time beforehand.

Jay's name is on our Web site as the "go-to" person for any questions, problems, complaints, suggestions. Well! He's been "gone to" so much by so many women, he's just plumb out of the mood for females most days! One afternoon, he demanded a meeting with me and his mom, Tammy, at our Official Conference Room—the outside deck at La Cazuela, our favorite Mexican restaurant in Jackson. Once the Official Meeting Refreshments (top-shelf margaritas and cheese dip) had been brought to our conference table, Jay slammed his work-gnarled hands down on the table and indicated, with a somewhat wild-eyed look, that he had that very day received what amounted to the Last Straw in the form of an e-mail from one of his many correspondents on the Web site message board. "They don't even address me—there's no opening greeting or anything," he sputtered. "They just launch right in with their demands!"

We just let him vent, bless his heart, and even encouraged him a little bit by asking what it was they were wanting that upset him so? " 'How do we make the big tits and butts for our outfits?' That's what they asked *me* today—just blurted it right out like that: *'How do we make the big tits and butts?'* Like I *know* or *care* how y'all make those ridiculous outfits you wear!" Tammy and I may not have presented as sympathetic a forum as he might have desired, which he probably surmised from the peals of laughter issuing forth from our gaping mouths and the ensuing mascara-stained tears streaming down our contorted faces and possibly from the repeated slapping of our meaty thighs as we gasped for breath and hooted all the more.

And that's when it struck us, me and Tammy, what a good thing we had done for this young man. If *ever* he had thought of marrying in haste, we have forestalled it, headed it off at the pass, nipped it in the very bud. It will be a Very Special Woman who finally gets our Jay. Possibly a mute woman or one who speaks a foreign language that he will never learn—but very, very special.

Okay, I'll get back to kids' birthday parties, if I have to.

Tell me this: When is the last time you set foot in a skating rink? Unless you have children, I can tell you when it was—it was when *you* were a child. No grown-up ever goes willingly to a skating rink. (Except for my good friend Jane Magee, who, at the age of sixty-something, was a floor guard at a skating rink and still has the best legs in her aerobics class, much to the continuing chagrin of the twenty-somethings.) The only reason for going to a skating rink is for a kid's birthday party. It would be fine if you could afford to rent the entire rink so that the only kids in there were in your party. With a small group, you might even dare to skate a little bit yourself. But no, when you get to the skating rink for your precious darling's birthday party, you discover that every child in your zip code is having a birthday party at the same skating rink, on the same day, and at the same hour as yours. The noise level alone is a major health hazard. With that, factor in eight thousand children on wheels and see what your chances of survival turn out to be. And what a shame you have to be so crabby at your own premature point of death.

Queen of the Night Salsa

All that is to say: I recommend that you plan a party that will force the other parents to remain on-site for the event. This will help ensure that the party doesn't drag on for too long. The only way to do this is to serve equal and liberal amounts of alcohol and salty stuff so that at least it will be bearable while it's happening. Toward the salty end, Anne Garrett from Greenville, South Carolina, suggests this delightful salsa served with really salty tortilla chips and massive amounts of Fat Mama's Knock You Naked Margaritas (see www.sweetpotatoqueens.com). We call it Queen of the Night Salsa. Here's what you need to begin your reign: **2 15-ounce cans black beans** (rinsed and drained), **1 17-ounce can whole-kernel corn,** drained, **2 large tomatoes,** chopped, **1 purple onion,** chopped, **$^1/_8$ to $^1/_4$ cup chopped fresh cilantro, 4 tablespoons lime juice, 1 tablespoon olive oil, 1 tablespoon red wine vinegar, 1 teaspoon salt,** and **$^1/_2$ teaspoon pepper** (I'd use less and use red pepper my ownself, but that's just me). You dump all that stuff in a big, festive bowl, cover it, and let it chill for a little while. Break out the salty chips and the 'ritas and knock yourself out.

Queen Angie from Oklahoma City wrote and told me that her very own mama had given her one of my books and, in return, when Mama turned fifty-eight, Angie ordered a whole big bunch of Fat Mama's Knock You Naked Margarita Mix for her birthday party. Angie reports that Mama "was so delighted she insisted that we keep making 'em until somebody was naked. While this particular wish did not come true, she had a birthday she won't (or maybe she already did) forget." It just warms my heart, truly it does.

FINANCIAL TIP

Here is a reee-ally cheap thing to do at parties—your kids' or your own. Go to Sam's Club and buy some big, giant rolls of heavy-duty aluminum foil. Serve a couple rounds of drinks to the parents and then whip out the foil and instruct everyone to make outfits for themselves. See, the great thing about that heavy foil is you can shape it into anything and it will stay put.

I take full credit for this discovery. Tammy Carol was moving to a new house and she invited a whole big lot of people over to eat and drink up everything in the old house so's she wouldn't have to haul it to the new one. As will so often happen when you have a whole big lot of people, a separation occurred—not by anyone's design, it just happened, and suddenly we found there was a group of *us* and a group of *them*. *Us* went inside to root around and see what hadn't been consumed yet, while *them* sat out in the shade by the pool. Malcolm White and I were the bosses of *us*. Malcolm was plundering the liquor cabinet and I was in the pantry when I saw it—a very large, unopened box of heavy-duty aluminum foil, literally thousands of yards of the stuff—and it just *came* to me, as the best ideas will do, and I hollered at Malcolm to come see, which he did. "Let's make outfits!" I said, and he never even gave it a thought—just snatched the box and yanked off a big sheet of foil and commenced designing.

That's when we discovered that you can make a thong out of aluminum foil. You can also make a preternaturally large codpiece. In no time at all, all of *us,* Tammy Carol included, had fashioned what we thought were extremely fetching outfits, and we decided that all of *them* would probably like to play, too, so out we pranced for what we considered their viewing pleasure and creative inspiration but turned out instead to be their ultimate befuddlement. Not only did they not want to join in; they didn't understand why we were so completely carried away over it.

So you will have to judge for yourself the nature and quality of the crowd at your party. Kids will love making aluminum-foil outfits, of course, but make sure they're old enough that you don't have to be making their outfits for them, which definitely cuts into your own enjoyment. If the parents are a bunch of *us,* by all means, whip out the foil. If you've got a bunch of *them* for parents, don't bother. But if you're planning your own birthday (or other) party, you might want to examine your guest list closely. A group of *them* will require a whole lot more money and effort on your part, while a group of *us* is way more fun and it just doesn't take booshitdiddly to entertain *us.*

We might as well face the truth: The only kids worth having a birthday party for are *us.*

12

Ho, Ho, Ho, Y'all!

I love Christmas—just love it. I even like
Christmas *shopping*. Nothing makes me happier than finding Just the Right Present for
somebody. For example, one of the Queens—
it could *only* be Tammy, who else—has been
beleaguering us all for *years* about her days as
a majorette and how she didn't have any hair
on her arms all the way through high school
from twirling that fire baton of hers, and how
grossly unfair she thinks I am because I won't let her
twirl her fire baton on the float in the St. Paddy's
parade. The prospect of us all jumping, in those
giant outfits, from a blazing inferno to the pave-
ment is not a pretty thought, that's why. I have

suggested on many occasions—to no avail—that she just *march* her little butt out in front of the float and twirl her brains out the whole parade route.

Finally, I decided I had to shut her up but good. So for Christmas I searched and called around until I found a Source— a woman who would procure for me an actual fire baton. It was hilarious. She was asking me all these questions, trying to determine what *size* baton to order, and we weren't really getting anywhere, so she finally just asked me how *old* my daughter was. I hooted and said, "Oh, she's around fifty," and it was pretty quiet on the other end of the phone. "She's a *former* majorette," I explained. "She's thinking of getting back into twirling, and the fire baton was always her favorite event." Did I want her to prep it for me, she wanted to know, or would Tammy be prepping her own? I told her I wanted that sucker ready to be set afire the very second she opened it.

When I went to the woman's studio to pick up the baton, the room was full of tiny little future majorettes with their first batons, all looking at me with awe as I carried out the baton with the ends wrapped in aluminum foil. Even in their extreme youth and twirling naïveté, they knew a fire baton when they saw one. I guess it's inborn for true twirlers. I resisted the urge to give it a little twirl as I walked out, an urge that would have been more difficult to resist had I had the foggiest idea how to do it, so it was pretty easy just to tote it to the car with no fanfare. Better to let those little girls *think* I was just waiting till I got it home and actually set it on fire before I commenced my frenzied maneuvers.

Ho, Ho, Ho, Y'all!

I placed the fire baton carefully on the car seat and went into the tobacco store, located so conveniently next door to the children's dance studio, and bought a can of lighter fluid and a Bic lighter. I wanted Tammy not only to be able to twirl fire immediately but also over and over again, without having to go out and purchase supplies—sort of like giving your kids a big sack of batteries to go with all the toys.

I wrapped it as carefully as I ever wrap anything, which is not saying much. It's not that I don't try to exercise care when I wrap things; it's just not believable that I *did* when you see the end result. Actually, I'd have to say that when it comes to gifts, my friends will tell you I am famous/infamous for two things: getting the right gift, first of all, but, second, wrapping it in such a way that it looks like I just fished it out of the garbage. Wrapping presents is not one of my talents.

I failed Scissors in the first grade—literally. I can remember having to stay in at recess day after day, to practice cutting out the funny papers with those little snub-nosed scissors they made us use in first grade so we wouldn't put our eyes out when we ran with them even though they told us *repeatedly* not to. I never did do it to Mrs. Alford's satisfaction. To this day, no matter what it is—fabric, paper, ribbon, anything that can be cut with scissors by any other human on the planet over the age of four— when I do it, it looks like I gnawed it with my teeth and that I'm probably missing a good many teeth.

I also cannot Fold—anything. I have no folding genes; all mine are wadding genes. I have observed some most excellent folding in my time. My former husband, the very neat and precise MoonPie, could fold shirts just like a French laundry. He could even fold *fitted sheets*. You should just *see* my linen cabinet now that I am in charge of folding the sheets—just so many big balled-up wads of cotton in there. I'm not even good at folding the *flat* ones, but I make no attempt at the fitteds—it's just blatant, willful waddage.

Wrapping packages requires both cutting and folding, and believe you me, neatness counts. So fine, I suck. Part of the fun of getting a present from me is seeing just *how bad* the wrap jobs can get, and it impresses and amazes even me to discover how much room for continued deterioration there is in that process. Every time we think I've done as poor a job as it is possible to do, I manage to do worse. Even for a reasonably talented wrapper, a baton without a box poses a certain level of dilemma. For me, of course, it doesn't really matter what shape or size the object is. I will swaddle it in paper, wad the ends up, stick 'em down with tape, and call it "wrapped." My wrap-job on the baton was so horrendous, no one could discern the true shape of the contents. This was a good thing. It didn't give any hints about itself.

I never give actual hints about a gift to a giftee, but when it's one I'm particularly excited about, I will talk endlessly for weeks in advance about how I have gotten them the very best present they'll ever get in their whole entire lives, cackling maniacally about it. I also give them my family's traditional hint: "It's BIG and ROUND and BLUE!" Of course, it never is, never has been, never *will* be big, round, or blue. This heightens the anticipation for all of us. I had Tammy worked into a fair lather over the prospects of her present—I had also informed everybody else in our immediate vicinity, so they were all pretty excited about it as well. I told Tammy that I had bought our precious George a five-foot-long blond Lady Godiva wig and that *her* present was even better than that. She was *wild* to know what it could be. What could possibly be better than that? Only a fire baton in my estimation.

Finally Christmas Eve came—as it always finally does after the usual seeming that it never will—and Tammy came by so I could give her the Present. I had already told her it was so good she could just skip the rest of Christmas, and historically speaking, when I say that, I mean it and I'm right. For instance, a couple of years ago I gave all the Tammys their Travel Hair as a Christmas gift. If you've ever seen us in person, you know that when we don't have our actual Queen suits on (which are very unwieldy and not as comfy as you might think), we wear our Travel Outfits. These consist of well-coordinated getups—sometimes our SPQ jackets, T-shirts, miniskirts, and majorette boots, sometimes SPQ rhinestone-studded T-shirts and sequinny/feathery miniskirts—and we always wear our crowns and our Travel Hair. Travel Hair is the best thing ever invented for us, since we're all Women Too Old to Wear Hair That Is Both Big *and* Long. It's a very large, fluffy, *long* ponytail that attaches to the top of your head with a banana clip and has a big bow on it. It will stay on through all but the most ambitious hair-tossing. It looks as real as anything else we wear, and along with our Queenly Shades, creates that youthful appearance we so love. Understand now: we don't want to *be* young anymore—we've worked too damn hard *getting* old—but we definitely want to *look* young. Sunglasses and auxiliary hair are a big help, but the Dark is still the best friend we've got.

Anyway, after the Travel Hair Christmas, when I tell the Tammys I got 'em a good present, they get all worked up. I had Tammy worked into a complete sweat-down before I actually let her open the fire baton, and boy hidee, when she saw that thing, she let out a yell that sounded like a sorority house on nitrous oxide. She was fairly revved up about the thing and immediately sprang to her feet and commenced twirling. She twirled the whole rest of the night, twirled all the way to the car, and the last time I saw her, she was driving down the road, twirling out the car window.

I must further report, however, that, as far as we know, *she ain't set that thang on far yet.* I'm pretty sure we would know it if she had. There would be burn marks *somewhere*, whether there was a bald, burnt spot in the grass or in her hair. She has finally shut up whining about *wanting* to twirl fire, though— that's something.

Another thing I look forward to at Christmas is Christmas Breakfast. My family has been having some version of this event for over fifty years. It started when my parents were first married and lived in Kosciusko, Mississippi, next door to another couple, Brock and Eleanor Reynolds. The two sets of newly-weds decided they would have breakfast together on Christmas morning. Daddy made the best biscuits, so it was an easy decision as to where the feeding would take place. It became an annual event—even after everybody moved to Jackson and started having babies. My sister, Judy, and I were born into the tradition and have never known a world in which there was no Christmas Breakfast. Even after the babies grew up, married, and had babies of their own, everybody would gather at our house *early* on Christmas morning and eat big piles of breakfast. No sooner were we finished examining our loot from Santa than it was time to put it all away and make room for the Reynolds clan.

This went on happily for umpteen years and then Brock, the patriarch of the Reynolds family, upped and died, and when Christmas rolled around that year, the Reynoldses were not in a breakfasty mood. For the first time in the history of *our* world, we were alone—just our family—on Christmas morning. Judy and I thought it might not be a totally bad thing: We could loll about in our pj's until the middle of the day and not have to put our Santy Claus stuff away, and we knew we'd still get to eat, since nothing short of his own death could keep Daddy out of the kitchen. So we were halfway looking forward to a lazy Christmas morning—until it came. We got up at the crack, as usual, to survey the mountains of gifts bestowed upon our worthy little selves, and when the frenzy ended, there was nothing but *time*. A big hunk of empty, quiet, seemingly endless *time*, tick, tick, ticking away very, very slo-o-ow-ly. Nobody to clean up for, nobody to talk to but each other, no news to catch up on, nobody to *share* Christmas Breakfast with. We looked at each other and went, "Huh!"

Everybody roundly agreed that Christmas Breakfast without Other People sucked, and the next year, we put out a call for orphans—friends who moved here from out of state who couldn't leave town for Christmas, friends in the middle of divorce, anybody who needed a place to *be* on Christmas. They were not hard to find. We invited them and they came. And they kept coming. They quit even trying to go home for Christmas; they just came to our house. They got remarried and brought the new spouses. They had new babies and brought them. Nobody would graduate, and we just kept adding more and more people. Champagne and Bloody Marys flowed, and Daddy would cook until people fell over in their plates. It was the best time of the year.

Then, shortly after Christmas in 1982, Daddy died. We started dreading Christmas 1983 right then. We actively dreaded it all year long. We had no idea what would happen. How could Christmas even *come* without Daddy? How could we have Christmas Breakfast without him? Even worse, we knew, would be that silent emptiness without a houseful of people, and that, we knew, would be truly unbearable. So we notified all the regulars that The Breakfast *would* happen that Christmas, even without our daddy, and that *we* really needed *them* to come this year. As much as they might have needed us in the past, we were counting on their presence this year to carry us through.

They came to Mama's house in droves, of course, and we all pitched in with the cooking. Michael Rubenstein took over the making of the Bloody Marys in a masterful way. He also initiated the now-time-honored Christmas Breakfast tradition of the Kissing Festival, which entails him swabbing the tonsils of every woman in attendance with his facile tongue. He also likes to do a *dip* thing with the kiss—like in an old movie. This was a great little ice-breaker for an otherwise tense occasion, as you might imagine, and quite the crowd-pleaser amongst the female attendees. The other guys were all pissed they didn't think of it themselves.

A good time was had by all, and we thanked everyone enormously for getting us through that very sad first Christmas Breakfast without Daddy. Mama and Judy and I agreed, though, that it was just too hard having everything be the same *except* for Daddy, and so the next year, we moved the festivities to *my* house, where it's been held ever since.

There's only me to do the cooking these days, so I start on Christmas Breakfast well in advance. Here's the menu: Champagne and Bloody Marys, of course (but I don't have to do anything about that—that's still Rube's job), Sweet Potato Biscuits, My Very Own Ho-Made Blueberry Muffins, Miss Lexie's Pineapple Casserole (see page 258), Grinning, Grits, and Grillades, and Egg Stuff That Goes in Tortillas. I'm gonna tell you how to make all these dishes so you can have your own Christmas Breakfast this year. All I ask is that you drink a toast to the SPQs and be very consciously grateful for every smiling face around you. Some of 'em might not be there next year— life just turns on a dime.

Sweet Potato Biscuits

My good friend Maurice Hinton was kind enough to share this recipe with me. (He could be of so much *more* help to me if only he would help me design new SPQ outfits. He is *the* best costume maker I personally have ever seen in the whole world.) I shared my recipe with our Official Chef, Chris Lambert, who is responsible for the absolutely dee-vine SPQ Sunday-After-the-Parade Brunch. Those who have been to that stellar event *know* how good these biscuits are.

Now, this is a Southern biscuit recipe, so there are no exact measurements. Biscuits being the temperamental creatures that they are, a whole lot of trial and error goes into learning the "feel" of good biscuit dough, so I'm just going to tell you your *starting point* and you'll have to fool with it in your own kitchen until you find the right mix for you. It will vary every time you make them yourself, too; that's just the nature of biscuits. It took me forty years to learn how to make biscuits. No matter what I did— even if I just used Bisquick—I ended up with crackers, not biscuits. They tasted fine but the consistency was more on the thin and crispy side than the desired fluffy. Then one day I just got up and decided that I *could too* make biscuits and I was by God going to, and so I did and I've been makin' them ever since. Part of making biscuits is attitude, I reckon. With that in mind, if you want these Sweet Potato Biscuits, just decide that you're gonna keep at it until they make you happy. This recipe makes about a thousand, so you've got plenty of dough to experiment with.

Start by boiling **5 good-sized sweet potatoes** until they get soft, then let 'em cool and slip the peelings off and mix in a **few cups sugar** and mash it all up. I have put as few as 3 and as many as 5 cups of sugar. You've got to taste the dough and see what it needs—you can always add more; taking it out is a bitch and, well, nearly impossible, so watch it. Do your regular biscuit thing of **4 to 5 cups self-rising flour, 2 cups shortening** (I frequently use butter—yum!), and **1 to 2 cups buttermilk.** Work your sweetened sweet potato stuff in when you're doing the butter and *don't* overwork your dough—that's how you get crackers. When it's of a consistency that's not sticking to your hands like wallpaper paste but hangs together in proper biscuit fashion, it's ready to become biscuits. If the dough's too wet, add more flour; if it's too dry, add buttermilk; if it's not sweet enough, put some more sugar in there. They're *your* biscuits, they only have to please *you*. You can drop them or you can roll them out and cut them.

Then bake them at 400 on an ungreased pan until they get browned enough to please you. As I said, it makes a big pile of biscuit dough, so what I do usually is bake a pan and see if the texture is right, and if it is, I go on and bake a bunch at the same time. If they need tweakin', I can tweak and bake another pan and so on until I get it right. None will be bad, mind you, and they will *all* be eaten with enthusiasm. Some suit me personally more than others and I eat those myself. You can also freeze any that don't get eaten on the spot. The main thing about making biscuits is you just have to take charge and not be afraid. Do not allow yourself to be intimidated by a bowl of dough—or anything else, for that matter.

My Very Own Ho-Made Blueberry Muffins

My Ho-Made Blueberry Muffins are gen-u-wine crowd-pleasers. I mean, have you ever met anybody in your life who doesn't love a warm, ho-made blueberry muffin? I would consider such an individual suspect if I encountered one. I like to make about a thousand when I make 'em and just have 'em in the freezer—way better, in many respects, than money in the bank. When you make these muffins, use fresh blueberries whenever possible. (The frozen kind work fine, but do *not* use canned blueberries.) It's hard to get fresh ones at the end of December, so what I do is buy a bunch of 'em when they *are* in season and just sling 'em in freezer bags and freeze 'em. I don't do anything at all to them, and that's probably against every food law in the world—I don't know—but I tried it once and it worked great, so I have continued the practice. If you know of some reason why I should *not* do this, please don't tell me; I am happily ignorant.

Get **2 cups of blueberries** (fresh or frozen), put 'em in a colander, and rinse 'em off, then let 'em drain while you do all this other stuff. (Do remember that blueberries stain everything and be careful how you drain them.) Now mix together **4 cups all-purpose flour, 1 cup sugar, 6 teaspoons baking powder, 2 teaspoons salt,** and **2 teaspoons cinnamon.** In a separate bowl, melt **1 stick butter** and add to it **2 cups milk, 2 beaten eggs,** and **2 running-over teaspoons vanilla.** Then mix the wet stuff in with the dry stuff and add your **2 cups of blueberries,** rinsed and drained, and stir it all up, but don't overdo it on the mixing—you're making muffins, not meringue. Spoon batter into greased muffin-pan cups. This recipe will make a bunch. I use the tiny muffin pans, and it makes 6 dozen bite-sized muffins. Yum.

After you put the batter in the pans and before you put the pans in the oven, get some **lemon curd** (I have also used lime with excellent results—you can order both from www. theeverydaygourmet.com) and put a glob (about ½ teaspoon) on top of each individual muffin cup of batter and swirl it into the batter a little bit so it doesn't all melt and run off as the batter rises. That lemon curd thing is a secret that nobody knows about and it makes all the difference, and now you know it, too, because I love you too much to let you make inferior muffins. Bake these at 425 until they get golden brown. I like them with butter and honey—or just plain. I expect you will as well.

Grinning, Grits, and Grillades

If you live in some poor benighted part of the world where grits are not readily available to the populace, by all means e-mail us at our Web site (www.sweetpotatoqueens.com) and we will see to it that you do not long remain gritless. Because for the next recipe—Grinning, Grits, and Grillades—well, you *gotta* have grits. First of all, regarding the grits, *do not buy instant grits:* They are an abomination and should not even be manufactured, much less purchased, cooked, and eaten. Do not further encourage the propagation of these pseudo-grits by spending real money for them. If we ignore them, maybe they will go away. You can slide by with *quick* grits if you are committed to being a slackass. I usually make a lot of grits. Just cook the grits according to package directions, and then at the end, put a **glob of butter** and **some milk** in them and let them cook a little more to get thick again. I myself prefer Jim Dandy grits because Daddy preferred that brand and served them to me for thirty years, so they are the ones that taste and feel right to me.

Now for the grillades—pronounced "gree-ahds," not "grill-aids," just so you know. I think of this as French for "yummy stuff you eat on grits," but I don't know that for certain. Grillades are a pain in the ass to make, but they are well worth it, I promise. Otherwise, trust me, I wouldn't fool with writing all this down, let alone cooking the stuff. Here we go: Heat about **4 to 6 tablespoons bacon drippings** and use it to sauté **2 pounds of thin meat** (it can be round steak, pounded tender, or veal or even pork tenderloin, but whatever you use, cut in into bite-size pieces). Take the browned meat out, lower the heat, and sauté **2 cups chopped onions,** **¹/₂ cup green pepper, 2 cloves garlic, 1 cup chopped tomatoes,** and **¹/₂ teaspoon thyme.** Now remove all that and add at least **2 more tablespoons bacon drippings** in the pan, stirring in **4 tablespoons all-purpose flour.** You are making a roux, so you have to *stir it constantly* until it's dark brown. Lower the heat and gradually add **1¹/₄ cups hot water.** Then put all your cooked stuff in there, along with **2 tablespoons chopped parsley, 2 teaspoons salt,** and a **dash of Tabasco.** Cook it on low heat for 30 minutes, then add another **1¹/₄ cup water** and cook it about 45 more minutes. The meat should be *very* tender. You are going to put some cooked grits in a bowl and spoon some Grillades over 'em and eat 'em up, and *that's* when the "Grinning" begins.

Egg Stuff That Goes in Tortillas

This next recipe has had many names over the years—catchy names involving *burrito* and other Spanish-sounding words. Nobody, however, ever actually calls it anything but that "Egg Stuff That Goes in Tortillas," except Mother, who says, "Egg Stuff That Goes in Those Flat Things." Making this stuff—even with the advent of such labor-saving developments as pre-chopped onions and peppers and pre-fab hash brown potatoes—is *still* way more trouble than I'm usually willing to go to. But where my favorite foods and Christmas Breakfast are concerned, I'm known to make exceptions.

One reason the Egg Stuff is so much trouble for me is that I quadruple the recipe when I make it for Christmas Breakfast, and making that big a pile of *anything* is a tribulation. For normal consumption, one batch should suffice. Brown **½ pound sausage** (I like Bryan Sausage, and I like the "hot" variety). Don't make it into patties; you want it all broken up. Drain it and set it aside. Then you can either peel and grate **2 large potatoes** or do what I do now and use **one package of fresh** (not frozen) **hash brown potatoes** (talk about your godsend). Put your potatoes of choice in the skillet with **1 medium chopped green pepper** and **½ cup chopped onion** (frozen ones work just fine, thankfully) and cook all that until it's done and the potatoes have browned. Then put in **2 tablespoons butter** and stir, add **2 cups shredded**

Pepper Jack cheese, a can of chopped green chiles, and the sausage. Salt and pepper it to taste. Now, here's the good part: This mixture will freeze great. All you have to do when you want to serve it (or eat it all yourself) is thaw it out. Then you scramble some **eggs** (8 for all of this at once, but I usually cook it in batches as it is eaten). When you pour the eggs in the skillet, throw in some of the cheesy-sausagey stuff and cook it until the eggs are done. Then each person puts some Egg Stuff in a warmed tortilla, adds a little **taco sauce** on top (I like the "hot" myself), and rolls it up and eats it. Everybody's happy.

All of these dishes freeze great, so make tons of it and freeze the extra. Then you can have Christmas any ole time at a moment's notice.

FINANCIAL TIP

The more money I have, the more I spend at Christmas—on gifts, on charity, on food. I don't care—I like it this way and have no intention of changing it ever, I love Christmas. If, however, you don't share my enthusiasm for all this, you can save a ton by becoming a Jehovah's Witness. It will involve some changes in your dress code, but just *think* of the money you'll save on makeup. You'll be doing a lot of door-to-door walking, but hey, you probably need the exercise, and the religious cold-calling is probably a great confidence-builder, which might come in handy for other aspects of your life. And by the way, you will need your confidence boosted somewhat if you start walking around in broad daylight with no makeup on. But even the Witnesses join in the fun at the after-Christmas sales. Between the sales and the no makeup/no Christmas shopping—just *think* of the money you'll save.

Tammy and I discussed it and decided that the no-makeup thing would be a deal-breaker for us should we ever consider embracing a fundamentalist religion. We couldn't decide which was worse—no makeup or a *bhurka*—and decided it was no makeup. As hot and cumbersome as a *bhurka* must be, at least your naked face is hidden from view. My good friend Shirley took up with the Pentecostals in a big way, but she would not give up her makeup. Shirley was gorgeous but she knew what we all know: Everything's better with gravy, and faces are no exception. We just all look better with a little something on our faces, and Shirley was of the opinion that if a little is good, well, then, more must certainly be better. Those church folks gave her fits over it all the time, too. She just stared 'em down and declared that "the Bible says they worked on Esther for six months before she was presented to the King, and you can't make me believe in all that time, all they did was put oil on her body. And besides that, y'all have got everything but the kitchen sink in all that hair and I don't see one bit of difference. God likes me beautiful, so there—leave me alone." But they never did, of course. Not even at Christmas!

13

New Year's Promises to Keep

I hate New Year's Eve—always have. After many years of being truly amazed at just *how* bad a time it's possible to have on New Year's Eve, I finally just gave it up and quit observing it in the usual fashion. Me and one of the Queens, Tammy, have spent our collective *best* New Year's Eves together at the Krystal eating those stinky little burgers. Tammy prefers hers with *extra* onions and mustard, which is difficult for me to even imagine.

Last year, our precious Jay (yes, that Jay—the one who runs our Web site) had a great New

Year's Eve party. It had a Prom Theme (we do love a theme) and he decorated his living room with a photo set that said, "Evening Under the Stars" or something equally hokey, and you stood in front of it with your date and Jay took your picture. Everybody wore appropriate prom-y garb. Jay won the prize in my book: He had on a baby-blue tuxedo with a ruffled shirt (blue ruffles, naturally), white patent-leather shoes, and a tiny top hat that would *almost* have fit an organ grinder's monkey. He was a Vision, let me tell you. His sister, the lovely Meg, wore one of her mom's (Tammy's) very old cocktail dresses. How old? you may well ask. She wore them to her own Engagement Parties; and she won't even *tell* how long ago that was. We gave Meg a tiara, of course, and she was Instant Prom Queen. All of us old folks dropped by the party, thrilling Jay's friends, no doubt. But we just had our pictures taken and then did the decent thing and left.

The only thing I enjoy about New Year's is the Resolutions: I love to write them. Every New Year's Day, I write a letter to myself and then seal it and stick it in my calendar in "June," at which point I'll open it and see how I'm doing. In my opinion, New Year's Resolutions should be something you really already *want* to do. Don't say you're going to exercise when you know you're not. Don't say you'll go on a diet; who're you kidding? Forget about changing any old bad habits; you're not willing to give 'em up. You know you're not or you would have done it by now, surely. If you think it really is a bad thing and you need to change it, try resolving to do that thing just so *much*, until you get bored with it and quit. Otherwise, quit beating yourself up for it. That certainly doesn't accomplish anything. And, by the way, *announcing* that you *know* you have a bad habit or a problem does not mitigate it in the slightest for those in your immediate circle who may be affected by it. I know you think it does, but it doesn't. It just annoys them because you've admitted it out loud and *then* you don't do anything about it. This makes sense if you think about it.

I've had quite a successful run of Resolutions the last few years. Once I resolved to take several vacations—and did. Last year, I resolved to have some plastic surgery—did that. Having some successes under my belt and feeling fairly confident about my stick-to-itiveness, I wanted to undertake something important, something that would have a major impact on my life, and I thought of just the thing. It's really a health-related matter: it's good for your heart and your complexion, as well as your soul and disposition. If something is good, you know my theory, *more* will be even *better.* Yes, I have firmly resolved to have as much sex as I possibly can this year. Not that there has been anything resembling a *lack* of it lately—happily *au contraire*—but I really believe I can do more, you know? I don't think I've been living up to my full potential and really giving it the ole 110 percent. At the risk of not being believed, due to some of my earlier writing, I *promise* to do my best this year.

But if that doesn't work out, my backup plan is to eat more. Just to be on the safe side, I thought I'd start with these two recipes, which are variations on a theme (you know how we love a theme!).

Not~Southern Junior League Yummies

This one was sent to me by Sally, who first made this recipe to take to a very hotsy-totsy cookie-exchange party with some Southern Junior Leaguers. She felt she was somewhat suspect from the get-go since she was of Other than Southern Extraction, bless her heart. She demonstrated True Queenly Traits, though. When she received the invitation, she was at a loss for a recipe to use, so what did she do but get the Junior League cookbook from her native (not Southern) state. She knew—rightly so—that she could not go wrong with a recipe from a Junior League cookbook—even if it *wasn't* Southern. I mean, after all, who knows food better than the Ladies Who Lunch? (Yeah, they lunch, all right, but they also work their asses off for their communities. I say we *buy* them lunch.) So anyway, Sally took these Not-Southern Junior League Yummies to the cookie swap and, of course, she was the Belle. They're, well, yummy.

First you get a cookie sheet (one with an edge) and line it with foil and then grease the foil. Trust me on this: *Line the pan.* Bring **1 cup butter** and **1 cup brown sugar** (don't make me tell you to use dark brown sugar, you oughta know that by now) to a boil in a saucepan and simmer it for about 5 minutes. Put a layer of **saltines** on the cookie sheet, close together. Pour the butter/brown sugar mixture over the crackers and bake for about 6 to 10 minutes (depending on your oven—pay attention) at 350. Remove and immediately pour **1 12-ounce bag of**

chocolate chips over the crackers, spreading them as they melt (doesn't it just melt your heart to think about it?). Sprinkle that with **¹/₂ of a 12-ounce bag of bits of brickle**. Let 'em cool to room temp and then chill in the refrigerator for as long as you can stand it. If you have managed to let 'em harden before sticking your face in, break them up into pieces like peanut brittle to serve them.

Sissie Mae's Sweet and Salties

Here's the *other variation*. Queen Sissie Mae from Plano, Texas, sent me this one, which somebody had given to *her* at the Kentucky Derby. Here's how to make it: Start with the greased, foil-lined cookie sheet with an edge. Melt **1 cup butter** (*not* margarine, like *we* need to be told *that!*) in a saucepan. Add **1 cup sugar** and stir slightly. Bring the mixture to a boil and let it boil for 4 minutes *without stirring* (Sissie Mae says she knows this sounds weird, but just keep the heat on low enough that it won't burn and do what she says). Pour this mixture over **saltines** that are spread over the greasy, foiled cookie sheet. Bake at 350 for 6 minutes (she is adamant about this, 6 minutes and *no longer*). While they're in the oven, mix together **1 10-ounce bag of peanut butter chips** (*not* Reese's Pieces) and **1 6-ounce bag of chocolate chips**. As soon as the crackers come out of the oven, dump all the chips on top. Let the stuff sit for about 10 minutes and then kinda smear the melted goo around evenly. Let it cool to room temp and then put it in the fridge, again, preferably until they get hard, but just do the best you can with the whole patience thing—sorry, we are no help at all in this department.

Third Time's a Charm

And when Cutie Pie and I were in Port St. Joe, Florida, lolling about in the May family's beach house, our lolling was greatly enhanced by yet *another* variation on this theme: Same cooking method but use **1 cup butter, 1 cup dark brown sugar,** and **1 12-ounce bag of Nestle's chocolate chips.** These are really three entirely different tastes. You'll probably want to make *all* of 'em every time, just to have it all covered. I know I will.

A *very* interesting study crossed my desk recently. I know you'll find it every bit as riveting as did I. It came to me indirectly, actually: Frances Lowther at the Page and Palette Bookstore in Fairhope, Alabama, gave it to the Cutest Boy in the World— who looks even younger than he actually is and you'll see why in just a minute—and then it was given to *me* by the Cutest Boy in the World, whose motives were admittedly (and happily) somewhat less than pure. This study states emphatically that having sex *all* the time will make you look up to twelve years younger. Yeah, uh-huh, it was in the *Reader's Digest,* so you know it's practically gospel. This psychologist, David Weeks, did a study over *ten years* (he was into this) where he had graduate students look at thousands of photos of men and women who were forty-five to fifty-five years old. The ones who the students picked out as looking the youngest—by up to *twelve years less* than their actual ages—were the ones who said they'd been having gobs of sex. Dr. Weeks said he reckoned it was on account of the fact that lovemaking revs up the hormones that reduce fatty tissue and increase lean muscle—making us look younger. Me, I'da just figgered it was the constant grinning, but I'm no scientist. But if I had ever been tempted to waver in the keeping of my Resolution, I am firm in my resolve now.

FINANCIAL TIP

We can all save countless thousands of dollars on plastic surgery just by having sex round the clock. Hey, it's cheap and definitely worth a try. And here's another angle on this thing: If you are currently in possession of a Man Who Can Pay for Things and he's suddenly going to be getting massive amounts of sex *and* he's not going to be presented with a pile of plastic surgery bills, doesn't that automatically free up a big pile of money for him to spend on you in other ways? Of course it does. Now, see? You've got to stay on top of your finances at all times and be on the lookout for these windfall profit opportunities.

14

A Few New Twists for February

February brings several days that call for celebration. One of the Queens, Tammy—Tammy Pippa, actually—has a birthday on the seventh. She generally begins carrying on about it around January 15, and we usually can't get her to quit milking it until the time the parade rolls around mid-March.

Of course, there is also Presidents' Day. (We used to get two days close together in February instead of just one Presidents' Day, one for George's—that would be Washington—birthday and another for Ole Abe's, but somebody decided we could do with just one, and now most people have no earthly idea what this day is for.) It's a fine occasion because there's no school and no work for a whole lot of people, and every store has a sale on! I personally would like to receive gifts on Presidents' Day. And it would also be a good opportunity for atonement for any people in dire need of forgiveness for, say, forgetting Valentine's Day, which is the week before. Presidents' Day could be a sort of second chance for them, if they were smart enough to take advantage of it. (I think George would approve, since he cut down those cherry trees and all. Abe, too, on general principles.)

Let us talk about Valentine's Day for the scourge on humanity that it is, and of course, offer a viable alternative. V Day, or simply VD, may not have been invented by the greeting card/florist/jeweler industrial powers, but they have certainly availed themselves of the opportunity to cash in on it. And well they should; it's what they do, after all. And, by the way, it really irritates the crap out of me when people whine about the commercialization of holidays. How you feel about a holiday—any holiday—is intensely personal, and if you have a bad feeling about it, it ain't Saks Fifth Avenue's fault, and it ain't even Wal-Mart's fault. Those guys are *merchants:* Their sole purpose in *life* is to sell shit. They have not been masquerading as philanthropists; they want you to buy stuff from them and they're completely honest and aboveboard about that fact. If you don't like holidays, go look in the mirror—the answer's in there. Do what you need to do to get happy, but at the very least, *hush* about it.

But back to VD. I say it's a scourge on humanity because, whether it's a "real" holiday or not, a certain level of expectation (which is never actually articulated) has been created in half the population—this would be in the Girl Half. Because expectations have not been actually articulated (read: written down in longhand and stapled to their foreheads), this has created a corresponding level of fear and loathing in the other half of the population—that would be the Boy Half. They know they're supposed to do *something*, but they're not sure *what*. And you know what they do when they're not sure—of course you do: They either do the *wrong* thing or they do *nothing*, and it's a toss-up as to which is worse.

Mothers of Sons: You can help us all out by incorporating certain lessons into your precious boy's home training. For instance, start early teaching him to Put the Seat Back Down. Kacey Jones, official Songstress to the Sweet Potato Queens, has even written a song about it (you can get lots of Kacey's great stuff on our Web site), in which she recounts the manifold miseries of being in a relationship with a Man Who Doesn't Put the Seat Back Down, and she sings to the heavens the praises of the Man Who Does. Bill Bradley, one of the only men we ever *really* loved, has invented the Johnny Light (also available on our Web site), which serves many purposes. The two best ones are (1) it warns *us* if the seat's up and (2) it gives *them* a lighted target so they don't pee on the floor—again. But if you moms out there currently harboring sons in your homes will start *now*—get 'em a Johnny Light and nag, nag, nag—a whole generation of women could enjoy that whole generation of men without ever once falling into the potty in the middle of the night. This is your chance to change the world for the better, Moms—your legacy, if you will.

And you can also teach them how to do birthdays and Christmas and anniversaries—and Valentine's Day. Of all the mandatory gift-giving days (and there aren't nearly enough of 'em, if you ask me), Valentine's would have to be the easiest. How hard is it to buy flowers? Plain ole red roses will do, although additional points are given for yellow. Cards are *everywhere:* You can get 'em at the grocery store when you're buying beer, even. Personally, I've never been a fan of store-bought candy, and most of us are fat and don't need it anyway, so you can skip that. Help your son find a reliable jeweler—one who can be counted on to assist in selecting suitable sparklies. For instance, he must learn that earrings with an embossed card saying "genuine rubies" should never be purchased for a woman over the age of six. As a woman, you know how much happier your son's relationships with the other women in his life will be if he learns these simple lessons. It's as important to his future health and well-being as teaching him to cross the street safely.

Because of all the men currently running loose out there who have failed to grasp the rudimentary details of VD, however, the Sweet Potato Queens have declared that, henceforth and forevermore, February 14 shall be known as Worldwide Revirgination Day. Being personally, painfully aware of the pitfalls of Valentine's Day—whether one is in a relationship when the day rolls around or not—we think it is a good idea to spend this day in the process of revirginating oneself—just to be on the safe side. If he comes through, great. Who more than he will deserve to enjoy your newly revirginated state? But if he doesn't, well, you haven't wasted the day, and the Next Guy will benefit from your newly revirginated state, and we hope he will be more deserving of it. Win/win is all I'm saying.

FINANCIAL TIP

For guys—buying the stupid flowers when you're supposed to will be way cheaper than what you'll have to buy and do to make up for it if you forget.

Here're a couple of recipes for celebrating Revirgination Day: The first one is called Brigadeiras (I have no idea what it means; perhaps it means "My boyfriend forgot Valentine's Day and so I'm gonna eat a whole pan of chocolate"?) and it's from my friends Anton Cowl and Dirk Hoffman in Amsterdam. They toured the South on their vacation a few years ago and made a special trip to Jackson, just so we could meet at Lemuria Bookstore. I took them to Hal and Mal's, naturally, and ordered them Hal's gumbo (Hal White can flat make some soup now; doesn't matter what kind—he just aces it), a shrimp po-boy, and a bottle of Come Back sauce (see page 257). They were pretty happy. From Jackson, they just meandered through the South, driving and looking and taking pictures. Before too long, they were struck by, well, how *fat* everybody is in the South! They had never seen so many fat people before in their lives, and they became fascinated by our largeness, and soon the photos they were taking developed a theme all their own: big butts. Anton and Dirk started taking pictures of the Big Butts of the South, and that is really and truly where I came up with the title for this book: *The Sweet Potato Queens' Big-Ass Cookbook.* (But we didn't want it lumped in with the regular cookbooks, since it wouldn't *be* one. I suggested to my publisher that we call it *The Big-Ass Cookbook and Catechism,* but that just scared the water out of 'em, so I substituted *Financial Planner* and they came down off the rafters after a bit. So, thanks to Anton and Dirk for the title, and for this fabulous recipe.)

Brigadeiras

Get a good heavy saucepan and mix **1 can of sweetened condensed milk** (I love this stuff already!) and **3 tablespoons Hershey's Cocoa.** Heat that over medium heat, stirring constantly. After about 10 minutes of gentle boiling, it will start to get thick; turn off the heat and add **2 tablespoons butter,** stir it up good, and let it sit there and cool if you possibly can. Then while it's still warm, shape it into small balls by rolling between dampened palms. You can then roll the little balls in powdered sugar or chocolate sprinkles—or just into your *mouth,* which is what I opted for. This stuff is pretty perfect—only three ingredients and really fast to make—practically instant gratification. I made it once, being suspicious of it and thinking it might need a dash of salt or a splash of vanilla, but I was so wrong: It needs nothing but eating. (I did throw in a **couple handfuls of chopped**

pecans and thought it was very tasty, but this is strictly optional.) Anton added, "I haven't figured out yet how to make this one 'au gratin,' but I'm working on it!"

Love Lard

When Kelly Goley from Charlotte, North Carolina, sent me this one, I just howled. This stuff and the Brigadeiras would be the perfect things to wolf down if one finds oneself alone on Re-virgination Day—you know how we love to eat sweets and then salties. Kelly called these Bacon Wraps; I call it Love Lard.

Get a **pound of bacon** and cut the strips in half. Trim the crusts off a loaf of mushy **white bread** (Kelly points out that the crust has done its job and will no longer be needed). Cut each slice of bread in thirds and smear some **Cream of Mushroom soup** on each one and lay it down on a bacon strip. Roll it up and stick it with a toothpick. Bake these little delights at 325 for one hour. My favorite part of Kelly's recipe: *"Serves one!"* Tee-hee.

I've heard from thousands of readers about the two sets of Magic Words set forth in *The Sweet Potato Queens' Book of Love* and *God Save the Sweet Potato Queens:* the Promise and the Six Words ("Oh no, let *me* handle that"). Karin, an ER physician, wrote that on one particularly frantic day at work (you can imagine how frantic a day in a New Orleans emergency room is), she was searching in vain everywhere for an otoscope (one of those thingees they look in our ears with). Nobody would help her look. Everybody kept running around frenetically, until she finally just stood in the middle of the ER and shouted, "Who do I have to blow to find an otoscope in this place?" She said gleefully that the new and bigger chaos that ensued was most gratifying—men running up and down the halls, crashing into stretchers and walls, shoving each other out of the way. Very soon—very soon, indeed—she found herself in a veritable *sea* of otoscopes, and she thought to herself, "Aha—*this* is power."

Nancy from the Midwest wrote that she challenged her husband, Doug, to think of the Six Magic Words a man could say to a woman. He came up with an excellent set of his own six: "I love you—here's some money!" And she didn't even have to invoke the Promise to get that answer.

I received a most informative missive from a Ms. Glazier, who had given *Sweet Potato Queens' Book of Love* to a male friend of hers (clearly a fiancé, I determined from her letter), in hopes of educating him about the Promise. He had the strange idea that there are certain days of the year when a blowjob is *automatic* for a guy—like his birthday, for instance. On New Year's Eve, the two of them fell into the cocktails and it ended with *him* getting *her* calendar out and circling days on which *he* felt he was due an Automatic. Of course, there was not a single week of the year that didn't have at least one circle in it. Says *he*.

A man who claimed to be from Tomball, Texas (one of my favorite town names of all time, I gotta tell you), sent me his own list of the Five Women a Man Can't Live Without: One Who Cooks—and he wants one who can dish up plenty of manly food involving large, dead animals; One to Take Care of

A Few New Twists for February

Things—like everything basically, but especially everything to do with the kids and bank overdrafts and anything else that might keep him from watching hunting and fishing shows on TV; One Who Looks Good at the Office Christmas Party—the best trophy of all, according to Tomball's Finest, being one in a skintight dress ("like the SPQs wear"—surely he knows we're padded, bless his heart); One Who Never Complains—about the fact that the grass is butt-high on a giraffe and he's watching golf on TV, or about the fact that he's toting a second mortgage on a deer lease and a third on a bass boat with front *and* back depth finders, or about him wanting to fool around at four-thirty in the morning before he goes fishing (a good woman should just shop and not whine, according to him); and finally, One Who Keeps Her Promise—he thinks this is why we're out-living men by four years and climbing, and that men who're Not Happy at Home are most likely to develop a wandering eye and blow the kids' lunch money on hot redheads with big tits in tight dresses. I read his list, and I just don't know about his chances. Most women I know would be happy to do all the stuff he names, but certainly not for a guy who's in debt up to his eyeballs—for sporting goods—watches golf on TV, and threatens to cheat if we don't put out.

Queens from all over the world are yakking night and day on the sweetpotatoqueens.com message board. They had a thread going about what Sweet Nothings—three-word fantasies—they most liked to hear from fiancés and prospective fiancés. "I love you" was not mentioned. Here were some of the favorites: "Are you single?" "You're *not* forty!" (said with a strong note of sincere disbelief). "Need a massage?" "I'll cook tonight" (listed as one of the top three-word fantasies). One woman wrote to say that she just loved it when people looked at her twenty-five-year-old sister and said, "She's not older?" The number one, wildest, most unbelievable (way-more-than-three-words) fantasy was, "Darlin', I don't even know your name, but you are my fantasy woman. My private jet is waiting. Come with me to the Caribbean and spend the rest of your life lolling on the beach with me, drinking margaritas, and enjoying lots of other fun stuff that I'll whisper to you on the plane. Money is no object. Anything you want or need, just say the word. I want to dance with you all night long and make love to you all day. If something needs fixin', I'll call maintenance. If you want all your friends to come down, I'll make that happen, too. If you want to talk, honey, I'll listen with undivided attention, but if you want to be alone for a while, I'll just disappear until you need me." Whew! I had to go lie down after reading that one. I've filed it safely away under "Top Ten Things in the Universe Least Likely to Happen in This Lifetime," so I'll always know right where it is.

Our good friend Joy Emmanuel wrote that a guy friend of hers was whipping up enthusiasm for a new holiday he and his buddies propose: Steak and Blowjob Day. They were carping about spending weeks of blood, sweat, and consideration (did the act of consideration bring on the blood and sweat, I wonder?) trying to come up with something that will evoke just the tiniest smile from us on Valentine's Day. (This has not been my personal experience, but this is his story and he's sticking to it apparently.) They feel that there should be a similar day set aside on which we women show our appreciation for the men in our lives. Toward this end, they declare that henceforth and forevermore, March 29 should be proclaimed Worldwide Steak and Blowjob Day—a simple, effective, and self-explanatory holiday created just for their benefit. We don't have to buy flowers or cards or plane tickets or jewelry (not that we would have a man who wants jewelry—that's territorial encroachment), we just have to provide your basic big slab of meat and a blowjob. I have to admit, it certainly requires a minimum of effort and expense, and since March 29 comes *after* February 14 (even the slowest ones know *that* much), it may have a positive effect on their Valentine's Efforts, yes?

Fancy Taters

If you end up having to cook the steak your ownself, here's my sister Judy's recipe for Fancy Taters to go with it: Mix **1 tablespoon butter** and **1 clove minced garlic** and rub it all over the inside of a 2½-quart casserole dish. Get **2½ pounds Yukon Gold potatoes** (she says it matters, so get this kind), peel 'em, and slice 'em real thin. Put half the taters in the greasy, stinky casserole dish and sprinkle 'em with **½ teaspoon salt** and **½ teaspoon white pepper**. Cut up **2 tablespoons butter**, in little teeny pieces and spread all over the top of the taters. Now sprinkle all that with **½ cup grated Gruyère cheese** (yum). Then make another layer just like that one: taters, salt, pepper, butter, cheese. Now put **1¼ cup whipping cream** and **1 tablespoon all-purpose flour** in a small saucepan and stir it till it's smooth, and then put it on medium heat until it gets just-hot; don't boil it. Then pour it over the tater stuff and cover and bake at 400 for 20 minutes. Then uncover it and bake it for another 30 to 40 minutes. It makes from 1 to 8 servings, depending solely on your generosity at the moment. Judy says she doesn't like them left over; the butter becomes "obvious and 'greezy,' so don't make extra thinking you can eat them up in the bed tomorrow when nobody's around." I take my sister's advice in nearly every situation, and if she says the leftovers ain't good, I expect she's telling the truth, since leftovers are our favorite food.

Now, I'm fairly certain that all of us who've grown up in *this* country have, for as long as we can remember, heard the old saw "The way to a man's heart is through his stomach." But as we all know, if their *mamas* can cook, you gotta give 'em more than biscuits and gravy and Promises to keep 'em happy and home where they belong. I read with interest the story of a foreign-born housekeeper who was summarily discharged from her position when a concealed camera revealed that she was boiling her previously worn underwear in the master's soup pot—*with* the master's *soup*. Somehow she had become convinced that she was making magic juju that would make him desire her. (I can see how she may have gotten this idea: I mean, have you ever gone with a guy who *didn't*, at some point in the relationship, put your panties on his *head*? Why, oh why, do they do this? It should be on *Unsolved Mysteries*. Our very own Lance Romance adheres strictly to our "Never Wear Panties to a Party" rule and says that it applies to men as well: "Men should never wear panties to a party—except on their *heads*—and then *only* if they are serving food.") But back to our little cook—ahhh, it didn't work out at *all* like she had planned, and now she's out of a job with a pretty large black mark on the ole résumé.

FINANCIAL TIP

I'd say you'd probably be better off getting fired for stealing the guy's car than for boiling your underwear in his soup. I'm just not seeing any way to spin this thing into something positive. For future reference, if you are giving serious consideration to an on-the-job activity equal to or greater than boiling your underwear in your boss's soup to make him love you, stop and ask yourself the Three P's: Is it POSSIBLE? For example: Is there a man on the planet anywhere who would be rendered hot for you as a result of eating underwear soup? Is it PROVEN? Do you know anybody who's had good results from this? Is it PRUDENT? I mean, really, is this guy even worth the risk of screwing up a whole pot of perfectly good soup and landing you in the unemployment and/or deportation line *plus* dying all your underwear tomato red, which doesn't even look good on you anyway, and you can't afford to buy more because *you ain't got a job?!* If you'll stop and go through this simple drill, we think you'll make a much wiser choice in your attempts to lure this guy. For instance, you could make him this sweet tater stuff, made totally without underwear, and you could serve it to him—also without underwear. I'm thinking he'll go for it.

Praline Sweet Potatoes

Judy's good friend Anne Simms Pincus owns the New Orleans Famous Praline Company (you can order these on-line at www. sweetpotatoqueens.com). Now, somehow or other, Anne met up with the folks from the cable Food Network show *Food 911*, and they took right to her (as everybody does) and wanted her to be on their show. She said fine—she would make this incredible sweet tater dish made even more incredibly by the use of her very own personal company's famous pralines, but she couldn't do the meringue part of the recipe, so the *Food 911* guys agreed to swoop in and save the day on that score. This is the part that Anne did: Bake about **6 pounds sweet potatoes** at 350 for about an hour, until they get soft, and then peel them. (Anne says you can use canned sweet potatoes if necessary, but I can't think of any acceptable reason why this would ever be necessary.) Next, combine **2 sticks butter,** softened, **2 tablespoons brown sugar, 1 tablespoon Steen's Louisiana cane syrup,** $^1/_3$ **cup sweetened condensed milk** (nonfat, even), $^1/_8$ **teaspoon ground nutmeg,** and $^1/_4$ **teaspoon cinnamon sugar,** and mix all that up with a mixer until it's real smooth, then add it to the sweet potatoes. Then add **1 teaspoon lemon juice, the zest of one lemon,** and **1 tablespoon orange juice,** stirring it in real good, and then add **1 cup raisins** and **2 cups chopped pecans** and stir that in. Finally, add **8 ounces New Orleans Famous Pralines** (probably about six big pralines), broken up to be about the size of chocolate chips, folding them gently into the mix. (As tempted as you will be: Don't eat it now; it gets even better in a little while.) Bake it in a 2$^1/_2$-quart baking dish (covered with aluminum foil) at 350 for 45 minutes. Then let it cool for a little bit and top it with meringue and put it back in the oven just until the meringue turns golden brown. This will make 12 people inordinately happy.

FINANCIAL TIP

If you are still absolutely committed to cooking your underwear in *something*, I'd suggest using a pair of panties as a coffee filter. You'll save money on filters, of course, you'll ruin only one pair, and your risk of getting caught is drastically reduced, because there's not a man alive who *ever* empties the filter basket on the coffeemaker.

Family Vacations and Other Atrocities

Please observe a moment of silence as you read this for my most best friend, Allison Church, who has lost her mind and will no doubt be in prison for the rest of her life for committing multiple heinous acts of homicide. She hasn't killed anybody *yet*, that I know of, but it's early.

Allison is scheduled to leave today on a *family vacation*. And not with just her *own* family. This—we all know, whether we will admit it out loud or not—is lunacy, if not actually a fate worse than death. Allison's "vacation" is worse than even a car trip. She is going with her own husband, David, and their two children *plus* her husband's sister, Rose, and Rose's husband, Peter, and *their* children, which include actual baby-types. They are going from Mississippi to Yellowstone and Mount Rushmore, and they are going, all together, in a thirty-seven-foot motor home!

Doesn't it give you a chill, a wrenching feeling in your gut, just to think about it? Wouldn't you just rather be set on fire? I would rather chew on aluminum foil with this mouth full of fillings. I would rather perch pantless on a fire-ant bed. I would rather walk barefoot through a field of slugs. I would rather eat beets. I would rather let one of those big ole black hairy-looking spiders crawl across my foot. I would rather get a root canal. I would rather empty the cat box. I would rather eat canned biscuits.

I would not do it. I cannot envision anything that could persuade me. And I said as much to Allison. She totally agreed and said that, indeed, that had been her first reaction—flat refusal—told 'em just to go right on ahead without her, Godspeed and have a big time. But then everybody begged and whined and pleaded and cajoled, and she foolishly allowed herself to be swayed.

No good can come of this, I told her. *Why* do you think they're so desperate for you to go with them? They haven't always been this hot for your company, have they? I mean, everybody likes each other and family gatherings are reasonably pleasant, but have they normally been clamoring for you to pile up with them for days on end? Of course not. All they want is another adult, preferably a good-sized one, to help herd all those kids around.

Then she told me how long they would be gone. "TWELVE DAYS?!" I said loudly. You are telling me you could have had twelve days *alone* and you allowed yourself to be snookered into running a day care on wheels instead? You either *are* on major drugs or you *need* to be. We-e-ell, she had always wanted to see Yellowstone, she said, unconvincingly, even to herself. And you think you're gonna see it on *this* trip? You'll be getting one kid untrapped from the tee-tiny motor-home bathroom while somebody else is keeping another one from setting fire to it. You'll be working to keep your kids focused on trying to kill only each other instead of teaming up and plotting the demise of the other kids.

Allison, listen, I pleaded, you are as devoted to your family as anybody, and you have a better-than-normal relationship with your extended family, but let's face the truth. Even within a family unit, everybody goes to work and/or school and stuff; you don't just hole up with each other night and day. You don't do that with your own family, let alone other people's. This trip consists of round-the-clock, unrelenting, never-ending *togetherness* with each and every one of y'all, and I, for one, do not have a good feeling about it. A tabloid headline comes to mind: FIEND SEIZES HATCHET—SLAYS SIX!

Another consideration for me personally on a trip in a motor home with a bunch of people (besides the bathroom facilities) would be "What are we going to eat? And when? And *how?*" I've never been anywhere in a motor home and so I'm completely ignorant of the whole concept. It must have some redeeming qualities—you see enough of 'em on the road—but I just can't imagine what they are, and I cannot bear fast food. I like food that can be prepared fast—but at home, not where I have to pay somebody for it. If I go to a restaurant, I want to sit down and have somebody come to the table and ask me what I want and then go fetch it for me and clean up after me. I despise standing at a counter and craning my neck up at a giant wall menu. I will drive through a Krystal, of course, but that's different, and only for special occasions like movies and New Year's Eve.

My own personal idea of the ideal vacation would include as few people as possible. Me and BoPeep are the right-sized crowd for me. I also don't like to have much structure attached to a vacation—or activity, either, for that matter. And I like to be semispontaneous about it. Every once in a while we'll just up and run away for a few days. I highly recommend it.

So anyway, I'm asking Allison—who shares my views on food and most other things of any importance in life—"Okay, what about *dessert?* How are you gonna make Chocolate Stuff in a motor home?" It was a quandary, she admitted, but she had found an acceptable substitute for traveling purposes, a dessert that would satisfy one's deepest soul-cravings for fat and sweet and could be manufactured anywhere, anytime—with no cooking, no utensils, and literally no *thinking* even. *Hah!* Let's hear *this* marvel and I'll be the judge of whether or not it's a stand-in for the most holy Chocolate Stuff.

Motor Home Marvel

I'm not too proud to admit I was wrong to doubt her. I offer, on Allison's behalf, the dessert so easy, you can make it in the back of a moving vehicle; so simple, all you need is the briefest run through the smallest grocery store; and yet so incredibly good, nobody can believe what it's actually made of. I give you Motor Home Marvel. You take **12 to 18 ice-cream sammiches** (vanilla ice cream, chocolate wafers), unwrap 'em (Allison says this is the hardest part of the whole enterprise), and kinda wedge 'em into a pan—9-by-13-inch or bigger, depending on the size of the crowd and the appetite thereof. Then you punch holes in the wafers with a fork and you pour **Smucker's caramel sauce** over the top. Spread **Cool Whip** on top of that and sprinkle a bunch of **Heath bar brickle** over the top of that and then you eat it, unless you've taken so long putting it together that it needs to be frozen again for a while before you can cut into it. I had to admit it sounded easy enough to meet the most stringent requirements, but I had to taste it to believe it. I made her do it for me, and all I can say is I will never doubt her again. I still think she's nuts for going on this trip, but at *least* she'll have something scrumptious to console herself with—Being Prepared is important.

Lazy, Low~Rent, and Luscious Pecan Puddin'

I told our friend Joy Emmanuel about Motor Home Marvel and she declared she had a recipe that was *far* trashier than that one—even trashier than the Twinkie Pie in *God Save the Sweet Potato Queens,* if you can even imagine such a thing. And easier, too. Do tell, I said, experiencing equal parts skepticism and curiosity. "You buy a pecan pie," she said, "any kind of **ready-made, already-cooked pecan pie** and a **tub of Cool Whip**—that's all that's in it." Fine, I said, but putting Cool Whip on pie does not a trashy dessert make. But Joy had a trick lying in wait up her sleeve: "You moosh up the pecan pie with your hands until it's just a pile of crumbs." "The *whole pie*, you just moosh it up?" "Yep," she said, with the confidence of knowing she was about to flatten me with the next sentence. "Then you dump in the Cool Whip and stir it all up together—it's Pecan Puddin'!" Well, I had to hand it to her—that is one trashy dessert.

No~Pain, Plenty~Gain Coffee Cake

Allison Buckner—in the SPQ Wannabe Pecking Order, she would be second only to our Precious Darling George—gave me this fairly trashy recipe, which is yet another elaboration on the frozen Parker House roll theme—what a boon to mankind those things have turned out to be. She confessed that her friend Joan Grohe told her about it, which I thought was big of her; she could easily have taken all the credit her ownself and I'm sure she was tempted, in the hopes of possibly bettering her Wannabe status—so she gets extra points for honesty.

For this one, you take **1 package frozen Parker House rolls (24)** and put half of them (still frozen) in a greased bundt pan. On top of those, put **½ small package instant butterscotch pudding mix, ½ cup dark brown sugar, 1 tablespoon cinnamon, ¼ stick butter,** melted, and **¼ cup pecan pieces.** Then make another layer with the other half of the rolls and top with the same ingredients. Cover the pan loosely with foil sprayed with Pam, put a clean towel over that, and let the whole thing sit out overnight on the counter. While you sleep, the dough will thaw out and rise magically (if it rises up over the top of the pan, just poke it down—with clean fingers—and it'll slink back where it belongs). You can spring from your bed, pop the pan in at 350, and in about a half hour, you have got the sweetest, gooiest, yummiest, most fattening pile of coffee cake you could ever want. This one will not serve you well on your motor-home trip, but it is ideal for a *real* vacation—lolling about in your own home all by yourself.

The Queens' idea of the perfect vacation must involve cheese— I would have to say the Queens are fairly united in our Love of Cheese. Tammy called me one afternoon from Lemuria, our home bookstore and the Only Bookstore We Ever Really Loved. She was in complete hysterics and said she was holding in her hand a book called *What Would Jesus Eat?* Yes, I said, and what *would* Jesus eat? There's already been ample discussion— indeed, even jewelry created—about the question "What would Jesus *do?*" (Several Queens have written to say that, after having converted to SPQism, whenever they see those WWJD bracelets, they ask themselves, "What would *Jill* do?" which tickles me no end.)

But the question of what would Jesus eat was burning a hole in our brains. I mean, if *we* were God, what would *we* eat? Cheese! was the resounding answer. We just know that if we were any kind of deity, we would demand an unending supply of all manner of cheese. I wouldn't go so far as to say that we worship cheese; we are, after all, smack *dab* in the very *buckle* of the Bible Belt (see Biblebelts.net and get one of your very own), but if someone did actually build a Church of Cheese, we could qualify as the cheese equivalent of nuns, I'm sure. "We'll go *anywhere* for cheese" is a popular slogan amongst our fat little sisterhood.

So we read, with great interest and not a little drooling, the account of New York artist Cosimo Cavallaro's Wyoming Cheese House project. This guy claims to have already covered a motel room and the model Twiggy in cheese—although unless she herself has been eating a lot of cheese in recent years, it probably didn't take a whole big lot of cheese to cover her, so we were not impressed in the slightest by *that* claim. However, when Cavallaro was asked for some explanation for his cheese fixation (as if one were needed), he replied, "It's milk. It's life." And we knew we had found a Kindred Spirit, since we ourselves would not consider life worth living in a cheeseless world.

And that sent us flocking to our travel agent, Melissa, to find out the fastest, cheapest way to get us all to Powell, Wyoming's, Cheesefest, where they have not only the House of Cheese but also the Parade of Cheese and the King and Queen of Cheese! Just think about it: Only about a thousand or so miles away from us, they were getting ready for a parade with a queen, and this guy was already melting down ten thousand pounds of Pepper Jack—one of our very favorite cheeses—and squirting it all over an entire house. Well, we just had to be there, that's all.

Our enthusiasm for the Cheese House was apparently not shared by all of the residents of Powell, Wyoming. One in particular, the guy who was living next door to the Cheese House, was sorta cheesed about the whole thing. He said it didn't *look* like art to him and he was pretty sure it wasn't gonna *smell* like art, and he was whining on account of the whole thing was only like twelve feet from his actual bed. And so there you have it: Let the word go out—people in Wyoming don't care nothin' 'bout Art.

Well, as it turned out, our local paper didn't give us nearly enough lead time with this story for us to make suitable travel arrangements. They told us about it only a week ahead, whereas, with a story of this magnitude, we think they should have been alerting us months in advance. So we missed it and it's all their fault!

To console ourselves, we made this exceptional batch of pimento cheese, known Down South as Minnercheese. And we think you'll love it, too.

Why~oming Cheese House Minnercheese

Here's how we make it: Get about a **pound of extra-sharp Cheddar cheese** and about **half a pound of Pepper Jack**—either grate it your ownself in the food processor or buy the pre-grated kind (I personally like to buy big hunks of cheese and sling 'em in the Cuisinart—it's more trouble, but somehow the cheese seems better to me and that's important). Whatever kind you pick, run it through the Cuisi with a **cup of mayo**—now, down here, that means either Duke's or Hellmann's, depending on your grandmaw more than likely. Then you want to add a **4.5-ounce can of green chiles** and a **4-ounce jar of pimientos**. (I love those little bitty jars, don't you? I just have to *make* myself throw 'em away—I always want to keep them, they're so cute.) Okay, then get a medium-sized **poblano pepper**—get the seeds out of it, then chop it up and put it in there. Then all you need is a little bit of **sweet onion** (just about ¼ of one will do it) and **2 teaspoons Worcestershire**. Give all that a whirl and commence to eating it straight out of the Cuisinart—on crackers, your fingers, whatever's handy. I will admit to you here that I truly love to eat it on white bread with the crusts cut off—and I am not the least bit ashamed of that.

16

Gift~Giving Occasions for Spud Studs

Depending on your astrological sign, it may be desirable—even necessary—to incorporate some extra gift-giving occasions into your yearly calendar. This would be gift giving by *others*, naturally. For example, if you have a November, December, or January birthday, you may have found that too often Your Day gets lumped in with Christmas. If you have a February birthday, you might get shorted on account of Valentine's Day—and don't forget Presidents' Day. Easter, Memorial Day, the Fourth of July, Labor Day, Halloween—none of these poses a particular threat to your gift-receiving potential, but a few extra Special Occasions wouldn't hurt you none, either, I suspect.

In order to elicit any cooperation from the person (guy) from whom you've elected to receive gifts, you will first need to apprise him of the fact. You need to do this *well* in advance of the day you've chosen to receive said gift(s). Give your intended victim *clear* guidelines about the nature of the gift(s) you will be wanting to receive. If it is merely to be a flowers occasion, let him know. If there should be plane tickets involved, he'll need an itinerary—detailed, of course. You can't just say you want to go to Las Vegas; you might easily wind up there just in time for some big Game Hunters Show and Exposition. My good friend, the ever-darlin' Bill Brown, went to one of those hunting shows once and dutifully reported to me upon his return. Although he was completely carried away with the event, it did not sound at all good to me. He allowed that there would be two or three booths displaying $100,000 guns and all manner of camo and hunting accoutrements, and then the next booth would have sequined cocktail dresses. You'd have a couple more with guns and equipment and then there'd be diamond rings and other fine *joo-ry*. This, Bill explained, was due to the large numbers of Trophy Wives in the company of most of the attendees and, as Bill further explained, "Trophy Wives require a lot of *mainte-nance.*" He said this with emphasis, as if stating some immutable law carved in stone somewhere, like the Ten Commandments.

Humph! I thought and probably said. *Regular* wives require a lot of "maintenance," too; it's just damn hard to get any. Seems to me it would be a whole lot cheaper and simpler in the long run for a man to maintain the wife he has in a conscientious manner than it would be to trade her in for a slick sports model who can't cook. But that's just me. Anyway, as I was saying, give him a detailed itinerary so you don't end up at the gun show. If he's stupid enough to buy you a gun, you don't need to be with him; you'll end up in the penitentiary sure as the world.

If you've got a hankering for some new jewelry, you need to do more than tell him. You need to give specific instructions to the jeweler himself, but you already know that, of course.

For the ones who really are Hunters at Heart, by all means, give them something *impossible* to find—the more bizarre and unavailable, the better. This is much safer than having them go off to hunt dangerous animals in the woods with real guns, so unless you're holding an irresistibly good life insurance policy, give them something to hunt that doesn't require ammo.

For instance, I mentioned to the Cutest Boy in the World that one of my all-time favorite books in the whole world was *The Little Folks of Animal Land* by Harry Whittier Frees, which was published in 1915 by Lothrop, Lee and Shepard Company. It is without a doubt *the* cutest book ever published, and as a small child I was quite enamored of it. The copy I have had since I was little—which was my mother's before me—is in shreds. Hardly any of the pages are still bound, and they've all been liberally scribbled over. But I have carted this remnant of a book along on every move of my life and always kept it in a prominent place on my bookshelf.

We can only imagine how difficult it would be to find a *new* copy of a book, which was not widely published in 1915. This, however, was the task that the Cutest Boy in the World set for himself. Lord knows how long it took him and what hoops he had to jump through to get it, but get it he did, and you know what? He was as pleased with *himself* for his accomplishment as I was to receive the book. So you see—it makes *them* happy to hunt things down for us, and we should really give them ample opportunities to do so.

As I've said before, I have a fondness for monkeys. Even the word *monkey* makes me smile. My sister, Judy, and I have even trained her part-time dog, Otis (oh, he is a dog full-time but only belongs to her part-time, since she has to share Otis with her son, Trevor, and his wife, Ruthanna; but they're having a baby girl, so we hope to get more custodial time with Otis), to perk up and turn his head sideways at the mere mention of monkeys. If we act convincing enough in our excitedness, he will run around the house searching for monkeys. So far he has not found any, but we didn't expect him to. The day he comes back with one will be a *real* exciting day, I reckon.

Anyway, I was driving home one day, talking to Judy on my cell phone, and as I approached the intersection where I turn to go to my house, I saw, coming out of my street, a pickup truck pulling a flatbed trailer carrying the *biggest* monkey I have ever personally seen, and it appeared to be made of concrete. It took my breath away—literally. I could not even form words—I just started babbling and gasping for breath, until finally I managed to get out, "THERE . . . IS . . . A . . . GIANT . . . CEE-MENT MONKEY! IT'S COMING OFF MY STREET! I BET THEY'VE BEEN LOOKING FOR ME! IT'S JUST WHAT

I'VE ALWAYS WANTED! WHO COULD HAVE SENT ME A BIG, GIANT CEE-MENT MONKEY?" (Those of us of a Certain Age will remember the TV show *The Beverly Hillbillies*, on which the hick characters were always referring to the swimming pool as the "CEE-ment pond.") It was the best thing I've ever seen, just sitting up there on that trailer, bigger'n Dallas—but alas! The truck with the sensational simian cargo drove away from my neighborhood. The monkey was not meant for me after all. It was all I could do to continue driving, so blurred with tears was my vision.

I had no choice but to follow the truck, of course. As shocked as I had been by the sight of the monkey in the first place, you can't imagine my reaction when I saw where she (in my mind, it was a girl monkey) was headed. The monkey's new home was the lovely lawn of the lovely Maudi Nichols, in one of the most lovely neighborhoods in all of Jackson, Mississippi. As I later learned, Maudi had seen this giant monkey outside a pawnshop in Vicksburg, Mississippi, and she was as smitten at first sight as I was. Only problem is, she saw it first. She did exactly what I would have done—moved heaven and earth to acquire that monkey and have it transported to and transplanted in her very own yard. You cannot possibly fathom the envy with which I'm consumed every single time I drive down Maudi's street and see that big, giant cee-ment monkey just *sitting* there, luring me out of my car to pay homage to her. Everybody pays homage to the monkey now. She is adorned appropriately for every holiday and special occasion. I want that monkey a *lot*, and if there was any way to prize her away from Maudi Nichols—

short of larceny of the grandest sort—I would have that monkey for my very own.

And so it came to be that the Cutest Boy in the World had another little quest laid out for him—the Hunt for the Cee-ment Monkey. Success eluded him for quite some time, until one day, for what turned out to be no apparent reason, we had my car towed from Hot Springs, Arkansas, where we were visiting his parents, to Little Rock. I say for "no apparent reason" on account of, once they got the car to the dealership, this little-bitty redheaded *girl* who worked there just hopped in and cranked it right up. This was a mystery of gargantuan proportions, as you may imagine. It would have been mysterious enough had some grease-laden mechanic-type guy managed to start the engine after a little peering, prodding, and head-scratching, but for this tee-tiny little ultra-fem girl to snatch the keys and immediately rev up the previously dead-as-a-boot automobile—well, the planets were careening out of control over it is all I can say.

After the tow-truck guy and the Cutest Boy in the World picked themselves up off the garage floor, and the little redheaded girl and I finished hee-hawing, Cutie Pie and I took our leave of the Volvo dealership and went to find lunch. We did find lunch, and right next door to lunch was a place that sold statuary—of the cee-ment variety—and so, naturally, I wondered aloud what chance in hell there might be that this place would have an actual cee-ment monkey? So in we went. Cutie Pie and I got separated almost immediately. He went to pee—so he said—and I struck out across the grounds, desperately seeking monkeys. What I found right off was a life-sized, full-color Mexican guy with a life-sized, full-color donkey—and I was fairly carried away with that, I don't mind telling you, but I recovered and got back to my monkey hunt. I did not find a cee-ment monkey or anything else worthy of note, but eventually I did find Cutie Pie and we completed our search of the grounds.

In the very back of the very large lot, behind a big pile of cee-ment dwarves and toadstools, I spied *something* that caught my attention. After much lugging and rearranging of dwarves and toadstools, *there it was*—at last—the object of my desire: a gen-u-wine cee-ment monkey. Now, granted, it was a small cee-ment monkey. Compared to Maudi's life-sized gorilla, it was a very small monkey, indeed, but a cee-ment monkey nonetheless. I was giddy with excitement, clasping it—heaving it, actually— to my bosom, shrieking and fairly dancing with glee. I was met, however, with a less-than-enthusiastic look from Cutie Pie. He was not shrieking and dancing with glee. He was actually looking askance at my monkey. Taking it from me, he pointed out that the monkey's head was kind of cracked-looking and its eyes were a little messed up and its banana was a tad chipped. This monkey was not quite all it should be, he thought, and he suggested that we continue our search. I protested that we had looked *everywhere* on this lot and this was by no means the first place we'd ever looked for a cee-ment monkey—without *any* success, I might add—and that this very monkey might well be the *only* surviving cee-ment monkey on the world market. But he insisted that we make yet another loop through the grounds.

Now, I knew for absolute sure and certain that I had not

overlooked a monkey, but he *is* the Cutest Boy in the World, so I humored him. But, of course, we didn't find another monkey, and so after a while, I said to him, "Don't you think we ought to snag that monkey and head on back to Hot Springs?" He just started hemming and hawing and questioning the wisdom of purchasing my monkey, and boy-hidee, did the alarms ever start going off in my head. I looked at him real hard and said, "WHAT IS WRONG WITH YOU? How can you be *undecided* about buying me a cee-ment monkey? I have to tell you, cute as you are, I'm having Serious Doubts about the future of a relationship with a man who cannot make up his mind about a monkey!" He then confessed that the only problem with getting that monkey was that he already *had* one in the trunk of the car, which he had intended to surprise me with, and that the woman who sold it to him had solemnly vowed that he had bought the *only* cee-ment monkey in her whole place. He was plenty disgusted that I had rooted around and found another one. And now I not only still have Cutie Pie but a very fine cee-ment monkey, too! My mother was somewhat nonplussed when I ensconced a cee-ment monkey in the living room of our brand-new house. The incomparable BoPeep, however, had no such qualms. She is nothing if not raised right.

The thrill that our own personal boyfriends/fiancés/husbands will enjoy finding That Perfect Gift for us can be shared by just about anybody who knows and cares for us at all—and isn't *that* good news? For example, I mentioned to our Head Sweet Potato Queen Wannabe, Precious George, that I would really like to have a sock monkey with long red hair. Since such an animal is not available for purchase anywhere on the planet, Precious George made one for me his ownself and presented it to me for Christmas. (The Maryland Crab Queens also brought me a very fetching Crab Queen sock monkey.)

Anyway, pick a day—any day you like—and declare it to be Special (deserving of presents), throw out the essential hints (instructions), and start planning the menu. After all, Your Special Day is a perfect time to eat a whole lot of wonderful and fattening food.

Enchanting Enchiladas

Enchiladas make us pretty happy. The sauce for these enchiladas is just the perfect delivery system for a whole bucketful of cheese—and so-o-o-o easy to make. The measurements are inexact, but it doesn't matter, it's pretty much foolproof (meaning that I am proof that any fool can make it). First, cut up a **whole bunch of squash**—yellow summer squash or zucchini, they're pretty interchangeable—and when I say a whole bunch, I mean a whole bunch, certainly several pounds of it; it cooks down to nothing, so you need to start with a lot. If you have never, ever cooked squash in your life and have no idea what qualifies as a whole bunch of it, pick another recipe. Then either cut up a **couple of onions** or use a bag of 'em already chopped. While you're chopping, heat up a great big skillet with a **few tablespoons of oil** in it and then fling the onions in there with a **few cloves of garlic,** and cook all this for a couple minutes. Then add the squash, cover it, and cook it for a little bit until it's tender. Stir in a **couple 4-ounce cans of chopped green chile peppers** and set it aside while you make the spicy sauce.

In a medium-sized saucepan, melt **4 tablespoons butter,** then stir in **4 tablespoons all-purpose flour, 4 teaspoons chili powder,** and **1/2 teaspoon salt** (you can put in 1/4 teaspoon of pepper if you want to, but I don't like black pepper). Add **2 cups milk** and stir it until it starts to get thick and then add *at least* **two cups shredded Pepper Jack cheese.** I generally use 3 to 4 cups of cheese because we *love* cheese more than air, but suit yourself, of course.

You just stir the sauce till it's all melted and then dump it into the squash. Now, you have to use some *judgment* here on how much sauce to add to the squash. You want as much as possible, naturally, on account of the sauce is where the cheese is after all, but you'll be eating this stuff rolled up in a flour tortilla—if it's soup, it won't work, so pay attention to how much sauce you're using. You can always freeze the extra or do like we do and eat it like dip on Fritos. Now put some **tomatoes** in there. If it is summertime, by all means chop up some fresh ones—a couple good-sized ones will be perfect. If it's winter or you live someplace not blessed with excellent tomatoes, use **1 or 2 big cans of chopped tomatoes.** Do *not*, under any circumstance, use some waxy, bland, hothouse tomato-facsimile, which is an insult to real tomatoes everywhere. At least the canned ones are red.

And now you are ready to eat. Warm a flour tortilla and spoon a wad of the cheesy-squashy stuff into it and eat it the best way you can—over the sink, if possible. The cheesy-squashy stuff will freeze, in theory—although I personally have never had enough left over *to* freeze.

Whatchamacallit Chicken

Here's something you can get the guys to do for you. It involves grilling—either over charcoal or on a gas grill—and that's a guy thing. The fact is it can be baked in the oven, but cook it on the grill because (a) it tastes better and (b) if you do it in the oven, *you'll* have to do it. Anyway, you get this vertical broiling device—it's just a little flat iron thing with two rimmed circles on it—and place a nearly full can of beer (or Pepsi or anything carbonated in a can) in each of the circles, and then you impale a couple of chickens on the cans. You cook it like that for a couple hours and it is just about the best chicken you ever had. The people who manufacture the device call it Juiced Up Chicken, and I've also heard it called Drunk Chicken and Tipsy Chicken, but Tammy Melanie and her sweetie pie, Brewer, call it Enema Chicken. You can get one of these devices on our Web site, naturally, and commence making your own Whatchamacallit!

Ray Lee's Tomato Cornbread

If you'd rather have your Whatchamacallit Chicken with regular side dishes like baked beans and the like, then, by all means, make Ray Lee's Tomato Cornbread, which is really almost too good for mortal consumption. Start by making a pan of **cornbread**—I prefer yellow cornmeal for this recipe—it just looks better, and as we all know, looks count. After you bake the cornbread, crumble it all up in a big bowl with a can or so of **chicken broth** (it should be moist but not soupy—use your own judgment), **1 cup chopped green onions,** with tops, **1 teaspoon black pepper, 1 tablespoon sugar, 3 heaping tablespoons butter,** and **2¹/₂ to 3 cups very ripe tomatoes,** peeled and chopped. (If it's the dead of winter and you're panicking for this, you can use canned tomatoes; you know it won't be as good, but it'll still make you plenty happy.) Put it in a greased pan and cook it at 350 until it's brown. (The consistency of the finished product will be more like dressing than cornbread.)

Now, after tomato cornbread, enchiladas, and Whatchama-callit Chicken (they are excellent with margaritas and/or Corona beer, by the way), you're going to want dessert, I know. I offer you one of my life's treasures, Lorene Caldwell's recipe for pralines. Lorene is the mother of Tom and David Caldwell (Tommy and Davee to me), who along with our best buddies, Timmy Glenn and Harry (Hogg) Hester, were my extended family for my entire idyllic Mississippi childhood. Every time I make these pralines, I am transported back to the Caldwells' house on Coronet Place, where in my heart I'll always be "rasslin' " in the backyard with my precious boys and Lorene will be in the kitchen, sneaking a cigarette when she thinks we're not paying attention, making a batch of these pralines. For many years now I have made these pralines at Christmastime, ostensibly to give to folks. I must confess, however, not one single praline has left my kitchen—not a one. I have personally eaten each and every one of them my very self, but my *intentions* continue to be good.

Lorene's Pralines

In a heavy saucepan, combine **2 cups sugar, 1 teaspoon baking soda, 1 cup buttermilk,** and **⅛ teaspoon salt.** Cook this on high heat, stirring it a lot, for 5 minutes, then add **2 tablespoons butter** and **2½ cups pecans** and cook it for a little while longer over medium heat. Then take it off the heat, let it cool down a little bit, and then beat it with a big wooden spoon until it's thick and creamy. Drop blobs of it on waxed paper and let it harden.

I guarantee that Lorene's pralines will make any day Your Special Day.

PART IV

Fine Food from My Big-Ass Buddies

Malcolm

Of all the people to whom I'm happily indebted for any and all success I've enjoyed, I owe the most to Malcolm White. In fact, a huge percentage of the fun I've had as an adult resulted from the imaginative ventures of Malcolm White. Malcolm is a man whose life centers around generating fun for others. In or around 1982, Malcolm did two things that changed my life (and a whole lot of yours) forever. He launched the now-world-famous Mal's St. Paddy's Parade in Jackson, Mississippi,

where we live, and he began publishing an irreverent newspaper called *The Diddy Wah Diddy*. Since jumping on Malcolm's bandwagon had always served me well before, I made
the leap to these two with no hesitation. I became the Sweet
Potato Queen in his parade and I began to write for the *Diddy*.
Now, twenty years later, Sweet Potato Queendom has come
into its own and I'm making a living writing books about it! For
these and many other things, I will always be profoundly grateful to Malcolm.

I am nearly as grateful to him for these recipes—food having the high, honored place in my life that it does! I am morti-
fied to confess, but confess I must, that in my whole life, I had
never actually known how to cook a pot roast—the dark brown
tender kind that you hardly even have to chew. I've loved it, but
it has been a mystery to me. I didn't feel *as* bad when I learned
that one of the Queens, Tammy, who owns a gourmet cooking
store (The Everyday Gourmet—theeverydaygourmet.com) and
who's a big-deal consultant for Viking Range and all manner of
fancy resorts and what-not, *also* did not know how to cook a pot
roast. Malcolm was ashamed on both our behalfs—pot roast, in
his mind, being second only to fried chicken as a suitable
Sunday dinner in the South. We had to agree and we hung our
heads at our grave shortcoming. So here's how Malcolm does it,
and you just have to imagine him talking in his low, slow,
Southern tones while moving effortlessly about the kitchen, just
sort of making food *happen* without ever seeming to. Malcolm
is not a bustler in the kitchen—he's a glider.

Malcolm's Pot Roast

First, he ambles through the grocery store, enjoying the scenery and blissfully anticipating the meal to come. Malcolm always loved to grocery-shop at the Jitney 14 in the historic Belhaven neighborhood in Jackson—it was everybody's favorite store; you could shop cart-by-cart with Eudora Welty, after all. Now we've lost our Eudora, and the Jitney 14 is not the same in too many ways to count. Sigh. So any grocery store will do. He selects a very fine **beef chuck roast** weighing in at about **2¹/₂ to 3 pounds.** He takes it home and he washes it off and pats it dry, then he takes a sharp paring knife and he pokes little holes in it on both sides and sticks fresh **garlic slivers** into the holes. Then he rubs the roast all over with **ground black pepper.** Knowing he's preparing the roast for loved ones, he treats it lovingly. He heats up enough **olive oil** to cover the bottom of his pot and browns the roast on both sides.

After browning it, he adds enough water to cover the roast and then he plops the following stuff into the pot: **1 large white onion,** chopped, **1 bunch celery,** with tops, chopped, **1 yellow pepper,** seeded and chopped, **1 bunch carrots,** chopped, **1 bunch parsley,** chopped without stems, **1 clove garlic, 2 tablespoons vegetable base (or 2 cubes vegetable bouillon), 2 tablespoons beef base (or 2 cubes beef bouillon), 2 tablespoons Mediter-ranean mix (basil, oregano, thyme), 10 shakes Mrs. Dash's Table Mix, original flavor** (Malcolm says the Dash Lady reminds him of his beloved aunt Glennie), **5 dashes Crystal Hot Sauce** (optional), and a **few sprigs fresh cilantro** (optional). He brings all that to a boil, reduces the heat, and cooks it forever or at least 2 hours. Once it is just coming apart with a fork, he puts the whole pot in the refrigerator and lets it cool off completely.

When it's cool, he skims the fat that's risen to the top, takes the roast out, and sets it aside. He removes about one-third of the vegetables and all the liquid from the pot and purees it in a blender. He puts the pureed mixture back in the pot and heats it with something to thicken it—he might use some **flour** or **cornstarch** dissolved in water or he might use **gravy mix**. He might toss in a snort of **red wine** for good measure. Then he puts the roast back in the pot and heats the whole thing until the gravy gets thick and the roast gets warm.

Malcolm perfected this at the knees of the many heaven-sent women in his family who hovered, cooking lovingly, for him and his brother, Hal, after their mama died when they were just little boys. If you've ever eaten at their restaurant (the SPQs' Official Restaurant), Hal and Mal's, in Jackson, you know that the lessons were not lost on Hal, either. They both learned by osmosis, having been blessed with three grandmothers and ten aunts—Myrtis, Voncile, Glennie, Coonie, Iva Rhea, Ida, Boots, Spoonie, Abigail, and Evan—who were cooking literally all the time for the boys.

Mal's Deviled Eggs

You couldn't grow up in a Southern house with as many gran-maws and auntees as Malcolm did and come away *not* knowing how to make decent deviled eggs. Malcolm loves a deviled egg and instilled that love in his daughter, Mallory, to whom he has been feeding his prize eggs since before she had teeth. "They always made her smile and still do," he says proudly. Of course, the smile has lots of beautiful teeth now since that baby's nearly grown. And I promise these eggs will put the same grin on your own face. You know the drill—boil some **eggs,** let 'em cool, and peel 'em. Cut the eggs lengthwise and put the yolks in a bowl with just enough **mayo, sweet pickle relish, salt,** and **pepper** to make 'em creamy but still bondable. Then you put the stuff back in the egg-white cradles. This is your basic "redneck" egg, Malcolm says, rightly. To spice them up for us, Malcolm will throw in any combination of **parsley, celery, green onions, cayenne pepper, Creole mustard, capers, olives, celery salt, dill weed,** and so on. He'll top 'em with a thin slice of **green olive** and **pimento,** a little **parsley** and **paprika,** and then he snatches a few off the platter and backs away real fast to avoid the stampede.

Malcolm has just bought himself the most wonderful house on the planet in Bay St. Louis, Mississippi. Cutie Pie and I went by to see it our last trip to the Coast, and as soon as we got out of the car, we said, in unison, *"I hate* Malcolm White!" It was the live oak trees on the property that evoked this overwhelming response. They must be a thousand years old: The limbs are bigger around than most good-sized trees, and some of them sweep down nearly to the ground before heading skyward again in huge, leafy arcs. The Spanish moss is thick, as are the honeysuckle, the ancient azaleas, and the mosquitoes. The air has a palpable stillness, the quiet broken only by the buzzing of the aforementioned bloodsuckers. We all hate mosquitoes—it's the natural order of things to hate them. But we also know that so many other creatures we love subsist on them, and so our slapping and scratching are mitigated somewhat, and the sound of their whine in our ears is at some level an affirmation that all is right with our world. Malcolm's new house has a surefire mosquito foiler, though—that greatest of all Southern inventions, a screened porch with a ceiling fan. Talk about all being right with our world. Our beloved Willie Morris used to say that air-conditioning and television were the great destroyers of conversation in the South today—so much of our culture is the spoken word, and sitting on porch swings under ceiling fans is where, over the years, many of our greatest words have been spoken. As long as there's one screened porch with a functioning ceiling fan and at least two people to sit under it, the South, as we know it and love it, will be safe. I'm proud that Malcolm is doing his part to protect and preserve our heritage. I noted with interest that the house also has a sleeping porch. Oh, swing down, chariot, stop and let me ride. Dear God in heaven, let me die on a sleeping porch with a tin roof during a rainstorm, Amen. Did I mention Malcolm's entire house has a tin roof? If I begin to die, would somebody please haul me down to Malcolm's and stick me out on the sleeping porch? If it's not raining, just put the hose on the roof and I'll pass on happily.

Bitch Meatballs with Sexy Red Sauce

Shortly before my peaceful passing, it's likely I could be a little hungry. Would you ask Malcolm to make his famous Bitch Meatballs with Sexy Red Sauce? It's possible this dish could raise the dead, actually. We call 'em Bitch Meatballs because, according to Malcolm, Georgia O'Keeffe said, "There's a bit of bitch in every good cook," or something to that effect. Malcolm got this recipe from Miss Mary Tuminello, whose family owned and operated the legendary Tuminello's Restaurant in Vicksburg, Mississippi. Malcolm says Miss Mary was a bitch in the very truest since of the word—a stickler for details, an impossible woman to please, not an easy sell, tough, strong-willed, and never willing to compromise—and man alive, did she *ever* make a mean meatball! As Malcolm says, "This dish is a *bitch!*" It's the dish that made Tuminello's.

Combine all this stuff in a big bowl: **2 pounds ground beef, 1 pound ground pork, 4 teaspoons chopped garlic, 1 cup chopped parsley, 3 slices bread (or a big piece of French or Italian loaf)** soaked in water and squeezed out, **$^1/_2$ teaspoon black pepper, 1 tablespoon salt, $2^1/_2$ cups Italian bread crumbs, 1 cup Parmesan cheese, 6 eggs,** and **4 tablespoons olive oil.** You then want to wet your hands and roll this stuff into $1^1/_2$-ounce balls (that's about the size of a Ping-Pong ball). Don't compact it too tight, because you want your meatballs to turn out soft, not like brick-bats, as Miss Mary was wont to say. Put a little vegetable oil in a skillet and brown all the meatballs all around; don't worry about cookin' 'em all the way through, they're gonna finish up in the Sexy Red Sauce and they will be plenty happy about it, too. The great thing about this recipe is, of course, that it makes about a million meatballs, which is just the perfect number, and whatever you don't want to put in the red sauce and eat right this minute can go in the freezer, and it's money-in-the-bank time. As Malcolm says, "One can never have too many meatballs." Amen.

Now for his Sexy Red Sauce. I'll say it's aptly named: If you don't feel at least a *twitch* when you read this recipe, you need to get your hormone levels checked pronto. Start by pan-frying **a few pork ribs, beef ribs** or a **small, bone-in steak** in enough **olive oil** to lubricate the bottom of a large stockpot. Malcolm notes that if you are a vegetarian, you can brown off some mushrooms instead or just start with the next step. Add **2 28-ounce cans whole Italian tomatoes** (hand-crush 'em—you know, open the cans and just grab the 'maters with your hands and mash 'em to a pulp. Malcolm *loves* this part, as do we), **2 6-ounce cans Italian tomato paste, and 1 15-ounce can tomato puree.** Fill one of the emptied 28-ounce cans with water and blend thoroughly. (Note from Malcolm: "There are many brands of canned tomatoes on the market from which to choose. I personally like Progresso or Contadina. The pretty, dark-complexioned woman on the Contadina can posing with a basket of tomatoes with the Napa

Valley—posing as Italy—in the background reminds me of my grandmother Atsie, who made a mean red sauce with sturdy meatballs.")

Add **2 tablespoons sugar** (Malcolm says this is optional— me, I'd go for it), **2 tablespoons mixture of dry oregano, basil, and thyme** (hey, now, pay attention—that's 2 tablespoons of the *mixture*, not 2 tablespoons of *each*), **4 tablespoons beef base** (remember, Malcolm tells us, this base has mucho salt in it by its ownself, so be sure you taste it before you go to salting it too much), **¹/₂ cup chopped fresh parsley** (Malcolm: "Hell, what I do is take an entire bunch of fresh parsley and pick the tops off, discard the stems, chop the whole bunch, and put it in the pot. The intercourse of the radiant green swirling among the voluptuous deflowered tomatoes creates a profound sight-and-smell sensation." Note to single women: If I were you, I'd try to drop by Malcolm's house when he's making this sauce—sounds like he'd be easy pickin's to me), **10 shakes of Mrs. Dash (regular)** (Malcolm: "I love that sassy lady"), **salt and pepper to taste** (taste *first*), and **¹/₂ cup red wine** (again, taste).

Malcolm starts cooking all that over medium heat, uncovered, and then in a separate skillet he browns off **1 medium onion,** peeled and chopped, **1 whole head fresh garlic,** peeled and chopped (Malcolm: "You can substitute the chopped-in-oil variety if you are a wuss"), **3 tablespoons olive oil,** and **salt and pepper to taste.** Sauté until the onions and garlic are the color of honey and then add them to the big pot of stuff and cook for at least 2 hours, stirring frequently and tasting constantly. Then remove one third of the sauce, puree it in a blender, and return it to the pot. (Malcolm: "This is a very personal thing with me, and you may well wish to omit this step. I warn you that I have burned myself more than once getting the *extremely* hot sauce back and forth from the pot to the blender, and sometimes the boiling-hot lava will erupt from the blender and splatter everything in the kitchen with deep red fire, so be *very careful if you attempt this dangerous maneuver,* and blend on a very low, slow setting!")

Malcolm's gonna take us home now, girls: "Now add your meatballs and cook as long as you can or until it's time to serve or you are so hungry you could eat the spoon you are stirring with. Add water whenever needed to keep the sauce the thickness of motor oil. Now crank the engine and call the guests to the table while you slip into the bedroom to change into something a little more comfortable." Whew! I'm needing to fan myself and think about baseball for a spell!

FINANCIAL TIP

If you insist on opening a restaurant, you *already* need lots of money for therapy to figure out what in the world is *wrong* with you. Malcolm (and any other restaurateur in the world) will tell you: It's just damn hard work *all* the time, and if you ain't open, you ain't makin' no money. If you are already in the business, here's what you can do. You're bound to have a bunch of drunk-ass friends who, just by the law of averages and their horrendous health practices, will not likely live to be particularly ripe. See if they won't let you buy a life insurance policy on them; you own it, of course, that's the catch. Buy some inexpensive term life insurance. They'll never live long enough for the premiums to go up very high. (This is also an excellent tip for women who are divorcing drug addicts.) It's way better than buying lottery tickets.

18

Our Precious Darling George

If you have read anything I've ever written, then you already know who Our Precious Darling George is: He's our precious, darling George Ewing, the Head Wannabe of the Sweet Potato Queens. He's the one you see at each and every parade in his green sequined shorts (with the big butt built in just like ours), and if *one* more person tells me how great-looking his legs are, I'll just puke. Like you think we haven't noticed his legs? They are too fabulous for words and they are *our* rightful legs. If *we* had such legs, we would be rich and famous for them. If *we* had his legs, we would most definitely make our official outfits be *thongs*—hell, we'd be wearing a thong to the grocery store if we had those legs. We would not ever wear pants, let alone panties. We would wear six-inch heels and fishnet hose and skirts up to there, and Lord knows, we would do some prancing around. But no—*we* do not have such legs, none of us. *George* has them—and he never lets us forget it, either. But then, we never let him forget that he's a Wannabe, either. It's the only power we wield and we wield it like an anvil on a rope. But as I said, George is not just *a* Wannabe, he is *the* Wannabe—the *head* Wannabe. As such, he is the Boss of Everything on the Ground That Has to Do with the Sweet Potato Queens at Mal's St. Paddy's Parade—all the Wannabes, the Spud Studs, the Tater Tots, the Queen Mothers, the Security Staff. Everything and everybody *not* on our actual float, George is in charge of. Naturally, I my ownself am in charge of everything and everybody *on* the float—I wield that power like the anvil on a rope, too, except maybe not so gently.

As the Head Wannabe, he does every single little thing for us (except for that One Thing: He doesn't love us That Way, but in every other way, he is utterly devoted). He builds our float, he paints our boots, he repairs the zippers on our outfits when we have gained too much weight to fit in 'em anymore, he makes us jewelry. He says, "Oh, no, let *me* handle that" all the time, and then he handles whatever it is without us ever having to even think about it again. He tells us we are beautiful all the time. He is completely loyal: loves those who we love, hates those we hate—on demand, with no notice. And he cooks for us! Whenever there is an occasion—and often when there's not—George can be counted on to show up with a truckload of home-cooked dee-lights. *And* the appropriate serving pieces. He sets a table—of course, he brings the flowers, too, and makes arrangements (that would make Martha go mad). He makes sure that everybody is served and happy—he never sits down himself—and then he cleans it all up better than it was when he got here. Yes, George Ewing is the Only Man I Ever *Really* Loved, and no, you may *not* have his number, and don't let me see you talking to him at the parade, either. He is *mine*, you bitches, you cannot have him. I will, however, share some of his yummy recipes with you. Of course, they won't be as good when you have to make them *yourself,* but you can just imagine how divine it is for me when George makes them with his own little hands and serves them to me on the good silver.

Queen Dip

George has made us this dip so many times, it's just called Queen Dip. He uses **3 6-ounce jars marinated artichoke hearts,** drained, **2 6-ounce cans crabmeat** (or one package of imitation crabmeat, chopped), **2 8-ounce packages Parmesan cheese,** shredded, **2 cups mayonnaise,** 1/2 **cup cream cheese,** softened, a **little bit of salt,** and perhaps a **dash or 3 of red pepper.** He mixes all that stuff together and just pops it in the microwave for like 5 minutes on high, takes it out, stirs it, and does it again for 5 more minutes. Then he puts it in a beautiful silver chafing dish with artfully arranged Town House crackers, but it can be eaten directly out of the microwave dish, with a fistful of crackers and you'll still be just as happy—more so if you don't have George to wash the chafing dish, which you don't.

Sylvia's Cheese Petits Fours

Now, George knows how we dearly *love* finger food—we like nothing better than to pile up on the couch with a big platter of finger sammiches and just eat and eat and eat. When the food is tiny, you can tell yourself you haven't eaten that much. George calls these Sylvia's Cheese Petits Fours, and our very own Queen Tammy Sylvia does love 'em—a lot. We all love anything that starts with **3 loaves of Pepperidge Farm very thin white bread.** Any child of the fifties who claims to not like white bread is a liar—and a fool, too, if she thinks any *other* child of the fifties believes her. You cut the crust off the bread—we especially love white bread with the crust cut off—removing any semblance of a resistive texture. Mix together **4 sticks of butter, 4 jars of Kraft Old English Spread, 1¹/₂ teaspoons Tabasco, 1 tablespoon onion powder,** and **¹/₂ teaspoon cayenne.** Sounding good so far, huh? Take 3 slices of the crustless bread and spread this goo on each side of 'em and stack 'em one on top of the other, then ice the whole thing with the goo like a cake and cut that little buttery cake stack into four pieces. When you have repeated this process with all the bread, bake 'em on a cookie sheet at 350 until they get crispy—about 15 to 20 minutes, but pay attention. Now, here's something: You can lay out these little cheese dears on a cookie sheet and freeze 'em, then toss them into Ziploc bags. And they will just be hanging around in the freezer, waiting to be popped into the oven at your next Food Emergency—like when somebody's husband has run off with a blackjack dealer from Reno or something. This recipe makes 60 so you can soothe yourself and a few friends handily.

Gorilla Casserole

George calls this Gorilla Casserole on account of it makes enough to feed a gorilla. This means it is maybe just enough to feed the Queens, which doesn't hurt our feelings in the slightest. We don't care what you say to us if *you're* doing the cooking, since we know you feel the same way. He just browns **2½ pounds ground chuck** in **2 tablespoons oil**, throwing in **2 cups chopped onions, 3 stalks of celery with leaves,** chopped, and **3 large carrots,** grated. After that cooks a little while, he puts in **2 2-pound cans Italian-style tomatoes, 2 tablespoons salt, 1½ teaspoons crumbled oregano, 1 teaspoon black pepper,** and **1 teaspoon garlic powder.** He simmers that for about an hour. Meanwhile, he cooks about **1½ pounds of macaroni,** any kind—it doesn't matter. He washes and drains the cooked mac and mixes it with **1 10-ounce package frozen chopped spinach,** thawed and drained, and adds the mixture to the big pot of meat stuff that's been simmering. He dumps all of that in 2 9-by-13-inch greased pans, then lavishes it with **Parmesan cheese** on top and bakes the casseroles at 350 until they get bubbly. The gorillas get misty when it comes out of the oven.

George's White Chili

When we've been really good—or whined a whole lot for it— George will make us a vat of his white chili. He gets a great big pot (we love stuff that comes in great big pots, don't you?) and, in about **2 tablespoons olive oil,** he browns 8 **boneless, skinless chicken breasts** that he's cubed (he says it's about 3 pounds' worth). This takes about 10 minutes; he just wants it lightly browned on all sides. Then he adds **1 large onion,** chopped, **5 ribs celery,** chopped, **2 tablespoons roasted chopped garlic,** and **2 more tablespoons olive oil,** and he cooks all that until the onion gets transparent. Then he adds **3 cans chicken broth, 3 cans white beans** (Navy, Great Northern, whatever—just white) with liquid, **2 cans white beans,** mashed, with the liquid, **2 4.5-ounce cans chopped green chiles,** $1/2$ **teaspoon celery salt, 1 teaspoon oregano, 1 teaspoon cumin,** $1/2$ **teaspoon chili powder,** $1/2$ **teaspoon white pepper,** $1/2$ **teaspoon cayenne pepper, 1 teaspoon salt,** and **1 package Country Gravy Mix.** He brings all that to a boil and then he puts a cover on it, reduces the heat, and just simmers it for a while, stirring every now and again to make sure it doesn't stick. Then he lovingly puts a Queen-sized dollop of **sour cream** in the middle of it, sprinkles the whole thing with a Queenly Portion of newly shredded **mozzarella cheese,** and serves it to us (in large, beautiful bowls) over fluffy white rice he has cooked perfectly. On the rare and totally odd occasion that any of this is left over, it freezes well.

George's Great Pasta Salad

George makes a really great pasta salad and we asked him for the recipe, and I swear to you, this is what he told us we needed: **1 pantry or cupboard, 1 refrigerator, 1 can opener, 1 really big pan,** and **1 really big bowl.** Open everything in pantry and refrigerator. Cook according to package directions. Mix well. Chill overnight. Serves a lot. Sigh.

Broccoli Salad

We did beat this broccoli salad recipe out of him, and it has actual ingredients and amounts and stuff. He takes **1 bunch broccoli,** florets only, chopped, and he mixes it with **1 small red onion,** chopped real fine, and **¹/₂ cup raisins.** He sets that aside, and in another bowl he mixes **²/₃ cup mayonnaise, ¹/₄ cup sugar,** and **2 teaspoons vinegar** until it's smooth and mixed up real good. He pours the mayo stuff over the broccoli stuff and stirs it up until the broccoli stuff is coated real good, and then he puts it in the fridge for a couple hours. Right before serving it, he cooks a bunch of **bacon,** the actual recipe calls for like 8 slices, but George, knowing us as he does, uses twice as much. (We know you feel just like we do about bacon: There's no such thing as too much.) He crumbles up the bacon and mixes it in with the salad. We think probably more kids could be taught to love vegetables a whole lot more if more bacon was added to them.

Lou's Slaw

Our Precious Darling George even made his precious, darlin' grandmother Lou Gill give us her famous slaw recipe—we love this stuff. Of course, we love it the *most* when he makes it *for* us, but we do so enjoy knowing what all is in it, just for the sake of discussion. First, heat together **4 tablespoons sugar** and **6 tablespoons vinegar,** and then mix it with **1 16-ounce package coleslaw, 1 cup canola oil** (you can use a little less), **¹/₂ teaspoon black pepper, 1 teaspoon salt, 1 teaspoon Tony Chachere's seasoning, 2 3-ounce packages ramen noodles,** crushed, **1 cup chopped pecans,** and **¹/₄ cup chopped onions.** You just stir it all up together and chill it before you eat it. It's really better if you can force yourself to leave it in there, unmolested, overnight; this is another reason it's better if George makes it for you—you won't be tempted to eat it before its time.

Fried Dill Pickles

Anybody who's come to Jackson for the parade has also gone to Hal and Mal's and had the Fried Plate—which includes, of course, dill pickles. It came as a great shock to us, here in the Deep South, when we first ventured out of our birthplace, to learn that *people in other parts of the country have never even thought about frying dill pickles.* We have no idea why they've never thought of it, since we, of course, fry *everything*, sooner or later. Fried dill pickles were just bound to happen eventually.

But here's what we've learned about people who come down here and experience this delicacy for the first time: At first they're confused and befuddled—fried dill pickles? They say this out loud a bunch while looking at the menu like it's written in a foreign language and they've translated it wrong. They say it over and over with a question mark at the end of it, sounding more perplexed all the time until somebody—from here—leans over and tells 'em, "Just *order* 'em," and they do. Oh, and then the look on their little faces when they chomp down on that first scalding-hot, crispy fried piece of pickle—it's an expression of Total Enlightenment. The fog has lifted, the veil is gone: They once were blind but now they see. And you don't see very many pickles on their plates for very long. Then they have to go home, back to the frozen North or any number of other places that are Not Here, and they are pickle-less once more. And for us down here, where we have Hal and Mal's frying up our dills on a very regular basis—well, even Hal and Mal's closes *sometimes*, so we understand these people's situation: You find yourself in . . . in a *pickle*, as it were, wanting fried dill pickles, wantin' 'em *bad*, and with no place to get 'em. Well, of course, *we* don't get in that particular pickle our ownselves, on account of *we've* got George, and *he* will fry us dill pickles his very ownself anytime we say. But for y'all who are not only pickle-less but George-less as well, here's how he makes 'em for us. He sifts together (yes, he has a sifter) **1 cup self-rising flour, 1 teaspoon baking powder, ¼ teaspoon paprika,** and **⅛ teaspoon red pepper,** and then he adds **⅓ cup beer** (he prefers Corona) and **⅓ cup milk,** adding them in equal parts a little at a time and stirring it together. He slices a whole lot of **dill pickles** and dips 'em in that batter, and then he fries 'em in deep, hot oil. He only turns 'em once or twice, just making sure they've browned evenly—he knows that even brown-ness is important to us, who are being waited on hand and foot.

Hershey Bar Pie

Now, I know you are saying to yourself: All the food groups are here, but where is the *chocolate?* You know that even George could not keep us happy for very long without giving us chocolate. Right you are, and, of course, he makes us chocolate—he loves us. He makes us Hershey Bar Pie! He actually uses a double-boiler (yes, he has a double-boiler, too) and he melts **6 1.35-ounce Hershey bars with almonds** with **16 marshmallows** in $^1/_2$ **cup milk.** (Since it's for us, he always adds **extra almonds,** and since you'll be making it for yourself, you'll probably want more almonds, too—I mean, why wouldn't you?) After that's all melted together, he lets it cool completely, which is hard to do without eating it, but do you want the pie or not? After it's cooled, he beats **1 cup whipping cream** and, Lord help us, he mixes it in with the chocolate stuff—be still, my heart. He pours all that into one of those crusts made of **mashed-up Oreos**—he makes his own, since it's for us and all, but you can buy a reasonable facsimile ready-made. You can then put more whipped cream on top—or Cool Whip. Since George has made his own crust, he's got some extra mashed-up Oreos and he sprinkles them decoratively over the top of whatever white stuff he's topped the pie with; we'll eat whipped cream or Cool Whip with equal gusto—we're democratic like that.

And now you can see why, even though his legs are *w-a-a-a-y* better than ours ever were and certainly ever will be, we just love him so. He *is* our precious, darling George.

FINANCIAL TIP

Money cannot buy a friend like George. If you've got one, you're damn lucky—don't do anything to screw it up.

19

The Queens, Of Course

I am frequently asked about the Sweet Potato Queens—as in, what are we like in Real Life? It may come as a shock to you that we don't wear those outfits all the time. Believe me, those outfits are the embodiment of the words "It's better to look good than to feel good." There is a direct correlation between how good they look and how *mizzabul* they feel. They weigh about forty-seven pounds apiece and it's all hanging off our necks, and when we take 'em off after a full day of Queenin' and *daincin'*, the grooves in the back of our necks are so deep, it looks like we've tried to hang ourselves backward. And did I mention that

we are plenty warm enough in those outfits? Think about it—
we've got on big red wigs, forty-seven pounds of fiber-filled
sequins, long gloves, suntan-colored tights *and* fishnets, socks,
and majorette boots. Thank goodness it's always a party when
we put on the outfits, as panties would just be unbearable.

The year 2002 marked the twentieth anniversary of Mal's St.
Paddy's Parade—and that is astounding to me. We were such darlin' girls when we started out, and I can remember being down
at Denk Drennan's beer warehouse working on the float (talk
about your perfect locations!), and one of the Queens—Tammy,
probably—turned to me and said with a big grin, "This is the
most fun thing in the world! Hell, we'll probably still be doing
this when we're forty!" FORTY she said, as if we would never be
that old in real life. Forty was something that happened to other
people, like your parents. It was not something any of us would
ever do *personally*. Well, forty has lo-o-o-ong since come and long
since gone as well for most of us, and ahhh, here we still are—
Queenin'! I guess we'll be doing it as long as we can pay somebody to wheel our moldy old carcasses out there onto the float.
And we'll just hope—as we always do—for good weather.

We've been truly blessed in the weather department, parade-
wise. It has never actually come a downpour on the actual parade,
or on our part of it anyway, and that's certainly the only part we
care about. It has rained *before* our performance and it has rained
after it, but it has never rained *on* it. The morning of the 2002
parade saw Jackson, Mississippi, under tornado *warnings*—not
watches (warnings mean real, live tornadoes are out there, not just
the possibility of them)—and we prayed our mightiest weather

prayers and, voilà (or as we say down South, VOY-OLA), long about noonish, the clouds rolled away and Mr. Sun came out and he shone and he shone and he shone down on our sparkly selves. And I'm here to tell you, we were *hot* up in those outfits! It got up to about eighty-five degrees—unseasonably warm for mid-March, even for Mississippi—and for a while there, we weren't sure we could last the whole parade route. (If it's nearly eighty-five outside, it's way over that *inside* those outfits.) Either we were gonna fall out from the heat or we were gonna have to find a place to tee-tee from all the water we were guzzling, and lemme tell you—tee-teein' ain't easy in all that garb. Peeling the stuff off is hard enough; trying to yank it back on is nigh impossible, and it will flat ruin your disposition, lemme tell you.

So, no, we don't wear the outfits very often. In addition to being less comfy than you could possibly imagine, they don't wear real well, either. Some have noticed (with no small degree of delight) the little changes that occur in the outfits as if by magic from year to year. They started out just plain ole green sequins, then there was some fuchsia lamé, then some fringe, then some maribou feathers. Well, I'll tell you what's up with all that. For one thing, of course, we do believe that More is More, and that whoever said Less is More was just stupid. We also believe that there is just hardly *ever* what *we* would call Enough. So we would probably be adding crap to the outfits every year, anyway—even if it wasn't absolutely necessary.

The additional froufrou has been necessitated by the inordinate amount of touching, stroking, fondling, and general all-around grabbing and rubbing that we are subjected to. Let's just say that people (men, as a rule) will take unbelievable (even for them) liberties with us outfitted Queens and, as a result, big wads of sequins have actually come off in the hands of our usually benign molesters and we have actual *bald* spots on our outfits that then must be covered and/or camouflaged by additional froufrou. But now we are running out of places to put additional froufrou, and even the previously added froufrou is starting to get frazzled. Touching, stroking, fondling, and general all-around grabbing and rubbing has not abated in the slightest. If anything, it's accelerated. We are in dire need of some new outfits is what we are, and we're looking for some kind of grope-proof fabric that can stand up to the stress from inside (as we get fatter every year that passes), as well as the outside forces visited upon us by overzealous fans. Well, I don't really mean *over*zealous. It's not possible to be *too* zealous about the Sweet Potato Queens, after all—just another area in which More is More and Better. (I wonder if they make titanium with a touch of spandex and a ton of sparklies?)

So, no, we don't wear 'em all the time, tempting though it may be, powerful as they are and all. We do just absolutely rule the earth when we have 'em on, and though that is our rightful lot in life, it can be tiresome. So we take off the outfits to rest a bit and to avoid being accused of taking unfair advantage of the common folk.

I remember when one of the Queens—Tammy, of course, but Cynthia Hewes Speetjens, the lawyer, in Real Life—tried her very first case in a neighboring county not noted for its progressive thinkers, shall we say. She dressed with such care, you would have thought she was going to her own personal parole hearing. I mean, that hair was slicked back, those earrings were nothing but plain pearls, that blouse was buttoned up, that jacket fit just so, those pumps were shined, the heels were of a no-nonsense height, that skirt was not a smidgen too tight or, God forbid, too short, and it had just the tiniest hint of an open vent in the back hem to allow for taking businesslike steps around the courtroom. She was as decidedly unsexy as it is humanly possible for her to have been this side of showing up in a flannel shirt and overalls, and she just absolutely got her ass kicked, lost the case bigger'n Dallas. She was sitting there feeling not great, as you might imagine, and the opposing counsel asshole saunters over to her and looks her up and down and kinda snorts and says, "Hmmph! That *slit skirt* didn't help you, did it, honey?" And, naturally, when she was relating the tale to us shortly thereafter—still wearing the maligned skirt that had, as I said before, only the *tiniest* little vent in the back (I mean, it wasn't two inches long)—well, we just went off and threatened to drive over there wearing some *seriously* slit skirts and beat the crap out of him, in the most no-nonsense, businesslike manner we could muster, but she demurred and took that oft-touted higher road. But of course, she never lost a case to the sumbitch again *ever!*

Lawyerly Taters

Now, Tammy Cynthia is aces in the legal department—quite highly regarded in this state and assorted others as an attorney-type person. On the other hand, as a cook-type person, she is feared, if not actually loathed, by nearly everybody currently living. I won't say that she *can't* cook—as she's a brilliant woman, she could clearly do *anything*—but she doesn't *choose* to devote her brainpower or precious time to it. So, when she went to a party at Bill Kirksey's office (another highly respected Mississippi attorney person who *can* cook) and ate this fabulous potato casserole, she was willing to do anything—including cook it her ownself—to have it again. Bill knew he had to tell her every single little detail of how to prepare the dish; attributing *any* level of knowledge, understanding, or expertise to Tammy Cynthia would be a grave error, and he knew it. When Tammy Cynthia sent me a copy of his recipe, however, as faxed to her by Lawyer Kirksey, I detected a number of glaring omissions right off the bat, so the parenthetical remarks are mine.

Put as many **whole unpeeled potatoes** in a large boiler as can fit. (Add water.) Boil until done. (When you can stick a fork in them easily, they're done.) (Remove pot from stove.) Place boiler in sink. Run cold water over potatoes until they cool enough to peel the skin from them (without removing the skin from your own personal fingers). Place (naked) potatoes in a (big) Corning Ware casserole dish. Set aside. In a (whole different) sauce pan, place the following ingredients: contents of **1 8-ounce carton sour cream, 2 bunches chopped green onions**—these are the long, green stem-looking things with the little white bulbs on the end—and **2 cups shredded** (Cheddar) **cheese**—you can now buy this at the grocery store already shredded. Cook down until ingredients are combined and pour over the potatoes. Mix thoroughly, making sure not to mash the potatoes. They will break into chunks on their own. Smooth it out. Place in an oven at 300 degrees for about 20 minutes. Once cooked, (remove from oven) sprinkle more shredded cheese on top of the potatoes.

Simple enough for Tammy Cynthia—tasty and fattening enough for all the Queens.

The year 2002 was special not only for being the twentieth anniversary of the parade. Much wonderment accompanied the installation of a new Sweet Potato Queen—a rare event, indeed, as all the many Wannabes can testify. It was decided (by me, naturally) that her extreme devotion to Queening in general, and to my own personal comfort and well-being in particular, had earned this former captain of the Queens' Elite Security Force, the ultimate prize—her own tiara and a coveted spot on the float. And so a new Tammy became Queen, but not before her Official Rite of Initiation, wherein she had to make the Promise to a high-muckety-muck from the local newspaper—in full view and earshot of all the Queens, naturally. Tammy has a very small shy streak, and activities of this sort, particularly when played out in public, just shred her very last nerve. The mere anticipation gave her hives—which, naturally, enhanced *our* enjoyment of the whole deal. Tammy, as Melanie Clement, Chief Financial Officer for the Ramey Agency, is used to a certain level of order and control in her life—all of which was relinquished in her successful execution of the Promise. In addition, she has accepted that her main job, like that of all the other Queens, is Whatever I Say, Whenever I Say—with a Big Grin and Proper Haste. It's a lot to ask of them, I know, but I like to think it is well worth their while. I can't think of a time when I have steered them wrong fun-wise.

At any rate, Tammy Melanie is Miss Smarty Pants Bid'ness-woman, and we are all so tickled and proud to have her as a Queen. She is perfect in every way—a little too perfect in some areas, if the truth be told, and I do intend to tell it as often as possible. For instance, her legs. The woman has legs that are nearly 'bout as flawless as our precious, darlin' George's legs. And it's just about more than we can bear, having her right by us on the float and all. I mean, at least we've got George down walking on the street, so we don't have to be right *by* him. Our plan is, of course, to fatten her up considerably before parade-time next year.

Since she does have this one little flaw that is so annoying to us, we particularly enjoyed hearing about one extraordinary problem she had one day. Tammy Melanie was busying herself with household chores early one Saturday morning and her little dog, Penny, was barking and whining to get out, so Tammy Melanie let her out and went about her chores. Penny, however, continued yapping nonstop in the flower bed directly beneath the window of the room in which Tammy Melanie was toiling. Tammy Melanie rapped on the window repeatedly and yelled at Penny to shut up, but Penny kept on yapping. Then Tammy Melanie went to the door and called for Penny, who either could not hear her or chose to ignore her. Finally, when she could stand it no more, Tammy Melanie launched herself off the porch and tore off around the house to deal with Penny up close and personal. Now, Tammy Melanie could not actually *see* Penny, but she knew where she was in the bushes. Tammy Melanie stood and called there again, through clenched teeth. Penny yapped on. Tammy Melanie then knelt and tried to tempt Penny in a more cajoling fashion. Still no luck. After trying any number of positions and tones, all of which availed nothing, Tammy Melanie found herself pushed over the very *brink*. So she simply charged directly *into* the bushes, impervious to the branches scratching her legs, arms, and face, reached down and grabbed Penny by the body, and lifted her up and over the leafy bushes. And what to her wondering eyes should appear—yea, verily in her own personal *hands*, but a full-grown, *equally* surprised armadillo! Penny—the dog—was still happily yapping on the ground beside her. Now, not many people, even in Mississippi, have ever actually *seen* a live armadillo. We all pretty much thought somebody just manufactured dead ones somewhere and, for some bizarre, unknowable reason, scattered them about our roadways. But I don't know *anybody* who's ever caught and held an armadillo with their *bare hands*. Now, granted, she didn't hold it very *long*—pretty much did the ole hot-potato number on his ass— but the indisputable fact does remain: Tammy Melanie caught that sucker with her own little digits, which she normally reserves for bean-counting, hair-fluffing, finger-food-eating, boyfriend-patting, and occasional bird-flipping. We are just so proud. As I've said *many* times, the "Sweet" part of our name refers to the *potatoes*, not to *us*.

Armadillo Hunters' Shrimp

Now, Tammy Melanie gave me this recipe, and it is *very* good. It's so good that when she served it to me, I figured she went and fetched it from Jim Hudson at Bon Ami here in Jackson and simply put it in her own dish to serve. I'm still not 100 percent certain that's not what happened, but anyway, it's great and here it is:

Heat a big nonstick skillet, throw in **1 teaspoon anise seeds** and **1 teaspoon cumin seeds,** toast 'em in the skillet over medium heat for about a minute, and then take 'em out and put 'em in a bowl for later. Next, in the same skillet, heat **2 tablespoons vegetable oil** until it's smoking and toss in **4 medium green onions,** coarsely chopped, and **2 garlic cloves,** minced, and sauté 'em over high heat until just soft (about 2 minutes). Then add **³/₄ pound plum tomatoes,** coarsely chopped, **2 medium jalapeño peppers** cut in rings, **1 teaspoon oregano,** the toasted seeds, **1 teaspoon pepper,** and **¹/₂ teaspoon salt,** and cook it for another 2 minutes. Then stir in **1 pound medium peeled shrimp** and sauté, stirring occasionally, until the shrimp turn pink; just a few minutes should do it. Then serve it, with lime wedges, over rice cooked with cilantro in the water or with saffron rice.

Corn and Peppers with Enhanced Fat Content

Tammy Melanie serves her shrimp dish with this superb, high-fat corn concoction. The Queens are unsurpassed when it comes to taking regular, *healthy* vegetables and turning them into little bite-sized heart attacks. Here's how you can do it, too. Heat **2 table-**

spoons vegetable oil in a skillet. Add **2 fresh poblano or anaheim peppers,** chopped and seeded, **1 small onion,** finely chopped, and **1 fair-sized clove garlic,** and cook it over high heat until soft (about 4 minutes). Then add **1 10-ounce package frozen corn,** ¹/₂ **cup light cream, 2 tablespoons cilantro,** finely chopped, and ¹/₂ **teaspoon salt.** Lower the heat to medium and simmer until the cream is slightly thick—about 3 minutes. It's a good thing she threw that cream in there; otherwise, this whole dinner wouldn't have any fat at all to speak of, and we can't be eating like *that*.

Bacon 'n' Eggs, Queen-Style

Vivian Neill—an actual *original* Sweet Potato Queen from 1982—has achieved our collective lifelong dream: She's an incredible artist, living in one of the most fertile places in the world for artists of all kinds, Oxford, Mississippi; she's gone back to school; her daughter, the beautiful Mallory, is nearly 'bout grown and so is nearly maintenance-free; *and* she's managed to *marry a plumber*, and a cute one at that (not that it would matter: He's a *plumber*). Now, granted, he's not actually a *practicing* plumber anymore, but he can still *do* plumber-stuff plus all manner of other manly things, and so Tammy Vivian never has to call or be at the mercy of any kind of home-repair guy. Now, if she isn't set for life, I'd just like to see who *is*. Sigh . . . It's just such a Cinderella story, we get misty just thinking about it.

Tammy Vivian makes a mean biscuit, I can testify, but biscuits by themselves have a hard time being fattening enough. So have some with Tammy Vivian's Bacon 'n' Eggs, Queen-Style. First, hard-boil a whole **bunch of eggs** (18 to 20!) and let them cool off. Cook **1 pound Bryan Bacon** and crumble it up. (Of course, this means you'll have to cook 2 pounds to allow for proper nibbling during the construction of this dish.) Melt **6 tablespoons butter** and add **6 tablespoons flour** and stir it for about 30 to 60 seconds. Then slowly add **2 cups milk** and cook it until it gets thick, stirring constantly. Let it cool off and add **8 ounces Cheez Whiz** (regular or the hot kind, which is what we like) and **8 ounces sour cream.** Peel and slice the eggs. Get a 9-by-13-inch pan, grease it, and put in a layer of the cheese sauce, a layer of egg slices, and a layer of bacon, repeating this and ending with bacon, of course. Bake it at 350 until bubbly. Eat it with the biscuits you made earlier or on toast or even an English muffin. You can assemble this ahead of time and keep it in the refrigerator until you get ready to cook it, but you can't freeze it, so don't waste all these eggs—not to mention the bacon—by trying.

There's one in every crowd, I suppose—ours is Elizabeth Perry Jackson, or Pippa to everybody lucky enough to also call her friend. Tammy Pippa is a commercial real-estate broker and she also owns and operates Back Road Architectural Salvage Services—or BRASS (the perfect acronym for Tammy Pippa's bid'ness). We love her so, but Tammy Pippa is our Bad Seed. She's just *bad*. All the time. You cannot *make* her behave—she is a full-time job. As you and everyone else in the world knows, I am *the* Boss Queen. I rule supreme and I'm not innerested in any input from much of anybody. And none of the Queens is even *tempted* to question my absolute authority in Queenly matters, except for Tammy Pippa, and she is just like any bad child you ever saw—always testing the water, seeing ju-u-ust how fa-a-ar she can go over any line before the insurrection is noticed and squelched. Tammy Pippa is always trying to sneak more rhinestone pins onto her costume and wear sparklier earrings than the other Queens; this is not allowed. Where she *really* flirts with danger though is in her unconcealed envy for my new Crown Jewels, handmade especially for me by Larry Vrba in New York. (He also makes the jewelry for another little organization—the Metropolitan Opera.) Larry made me a scepter, a bracelet, a ring, earrings, and a crown that looks not unlike the one the Statue of Liberty wears. All of it is absolutely dreamy. And Tammy Pippa dreams of it openly. Indeed, she covets it to the extent that I have to watch her constantly and often smack her little hands away from my jewel case or even my actual body.

Corn and Beans and 'Maters and Bacon

Whenever we have a gathering, Tammy Pippa can be counted on to bring something wonderful, but you'd better enjoy it while you can on account of she never uses recipes and never writes anything down, so you can never have it again exactly the same way. You know, here in the South, we do lo-o-ove our vegetables, and one time Tammy Pippa showed up with this combo of our favorites—corn and beans and tomatoes—with *bacon*, naturally. I just held her down and threatened to demote her to

Wannabe until she remembered, sort of, how she'd assembled it, so here is what I learned.

Cook **1 medium onion**, chopped, and **1 green pepper**, chopped, in a little bit of **oil**, until just tender. Combine **1 16-ounce can whole-kernel white corn**, drained, **1 17-ounce can lima beans**, drained, **1 8-ounce can tomato sauce**, **1 16-ounce can stewed tomatoes**, **1 tablespoon Worcestershire sauce**, and **salt and pepper** to taste in an 8-by-8-inch casserole dish. Cover the top with a **layer of bacon!** Bake covered for 1 hour at 350, but uncover it for the last 10 minutes so the bacon can get crispy.

Now, this is fairly yummy and can be done even in the wintertime when there are no real vegetables to speak of—certainly no tomatoes. In the summertime you can *use fresh vegetables* and ascend directly unto heaven with the very first bite. Cover the *bottom* of the pan with bacon, then put a layer of fresh lima beans (you know, those things take forever and a day to cook, so I always cook 'em separately for a little while beforehand), then a layer of sliced, peeled fresh tomatoes (just writing those words gives me a little tingle), a layer of chopped onion and green pepper, a layer of fresh white corn, cut off the cob (another tingle), another layer of tomatoes, and another layer of bacon on top. (Salt and pepper each layer a little bit.) Cover and bake it the same as the canned kind above and—omigod—you will just *die* over it.

Shut Up, Pippa, Tomato Gravy

Tammy Pippa is *insisting* that I give you this other recipe, and she, in true Tammy Pippa style, is *relentless*, and so fine, here it is, Shut Up Pippa, Tomato Gravy: Cook **sausage patties** in a black iron skillet till done, obviously. Then remove the sausage and put it on some paper towels to blot up some of the grease. Drain the grease out of the skillet, leaving only enough to coat the bottom, add a **handful of flour** to the grease and cook it, stirring *all* the time, till it turns brown; then add **about a cup of milk** to the browned flour and stir it until the lumps are gone and it's thick. Then add a small **can of Ro-Tel tomatoes,** drained, stir until it's the consistency you want, crumble up the sausage and add it to all that—and then spoon it over biscuits that you already made and turn around and slap the person next to you on account of it's so good, you just *have* to slap somebody.

As a group, we admittedly do discriminate—openly, in word and deed—against the Tiny. Our one concession to the Tiny Faction—and it's a big concession because she is *real* tiny—is our itty-bitty Queen, Tammy Sylvia. Most of the rest of the world knows her not as Tammy, the Tiny Sweet Potato Queen, but as Dr. Sylvia Stewart. When off-duty as a Queen, Tammy Sylvia is *fairly* busy. In addition to owning one of the largest funeral homes in the state, she serves as chairman of the Metro (Jackson) Economic Development Authority, a member of the board of directors of the Metro Jackson Chamber of Commerce, a member of the board of First American Bank, guest editor for the *Clarion-Ledger* newspaper, the first woman on the Board of Commissioners for the Jackson Municipal Airport Authority (she was chairman of the board for two years), first vice chairman of the Airport Minority Advisory Council, a member of the Commissioner's Steering Committee for the Airports Council International, a member of the First Flight Commission (in charge of planning the National Celebration of the Centennial of the First Airplane Flight of the Wright Brothers in December 2003), and chairman of the board of the Farish Street Historic District Neighborhood Foundation. Oh yeah, one more thing—in her *spare* time, she's a *practicing veterinarian*. I am not kidding. She does *all* of that, *all* the time, and that's not even really anywhere near everything—I just hit on some of the high spots. Just in case you're over there not sufficiently impressed with Tiny Tammy Sylvia, lemme just tell you that while she's been doing *all* that stuff, she's also been a single mom and has successfully battled cancer, not once, but several times, and has yet to drop a single ball. She oughta be the dang poster child for everybody dealing with adversity of any kind. So many—too many—people look on difficulty and disease as an excuse to lie down and do nothing but Be Sick. Tammy Sylvia chooses instead to look at all the stuff she's doing (and all of it's for other people and helpless animals, too—can we hear a Sainthood nomination from the floor?) as the reason she *can't* lie down and Be Sick. Tammy Sylvia is our hero, now and forevermore.

Tammy Sylvia was in the first graduating class from the Mississippi State University School of Veterinary Medicine (let's just say it was a few years ago), and she had gone through a divorce and was raising her son, Walter, all the while. We were marveling (as usual) at her amazing competency and energy, and we demanded to know how in the world she ever managed to get through vet school and live up to the constant rigors of single-motherhood. She said on Sundays she would load all her school books and Walter into the car and go to an abandoned mall parking lot. Whatever books she didn't need to be studying at the moment, she would put *under* Walter, who she put *behind* the wheel. Tammy Sylvia would study while Walter drove around—in circles—in the parking lot. Actually, it was just in one circle—he just locked the wheel and hit the gas, and he was happy, he was *driving!* Understandably, Tammy Sylvia is still not a big fan of the Tilt-a-Whirl to this very day.

Doritos and Hot Sauce

But Tammy Sylvia *is* a vet and she helped found the Animal Emergency Clinic in Jackson in 1982. Working long, late nights, she needs "a little something" (that's our favorite food) to keep her humming for a few more hours after she finishes with her last patient, when she puts on her puppy-dog fluffy slippers and settles back in her grandfather's old red leather recliner to wait for the next emergency. With nothing open for miles around her but the filling station across the street, well, the pickin's were slim at best. What Tammy Sylvia came up with was Doritos and Hot Sauce, literally. To this very day, her favorite comfort food is this: 1 *large bag* **Doritos nacho cheese tortilla chips** and **1 6-ounce bottle Original Louisiana Hot Sauce.** To go with this dish, she picks up 1 6-pack **Diet Pepsi,** and **1 roll of paper towels.** The woman will dump those Doritos in a bowl, cover 'em with hot sauce, and eat the whole thing while guzzling very, *very* cold Diet Pepsi. And she is just as happy as a pig in the sunshine.

Sylvia's Stoveless Black Beans

The Doritos and hot sauce qualify as "cooking" for Tammy Sylvia. Oh, don't misunderstand: She *can* cook; she just doesn't want to. Personally, now, I have never *seen* the woman cook— nor have I heard anyone *tell* of her havin' cooked. What I heard from her own lips is that she uses her stove as a planter, and I, for one, believe her. But she swears she will on occasion take the plants off the stove and cook for days, as if in some kind of cookin' *fit*, and then much time will pass (years) before another spell lands on her, causing her to cook on the stove.

Sylvia loves black beans and she's figured out how to cook 'em in her Crockpot, leaving the stove/planter intact. To make Sylvia's Stoveless Black Beans, you need a *big* Crockpot. Then start with **2 pounds of smoked neck bones** for flavor. Now, if you're not from the South, you don't have any idea what that means—but Down Here, we can buy smoked chicken necks in any decent grocery store, and they make for yummy seasoning. If you find yourself Up There, I suppose you'll just have to use ham or something else—I don't know. If I were you, I'd just move Down Here to make it easier on yourself. Then add **2 packages dried black beans** (Sylvia tells us they are two for a dollar at Wal-Mart!), **1 large onion,** finely chopped, **2 bay leaves,**

lots of crushed red pepper, and **lots of Sylvia's Special Seasoning**—which has nothing to do with Tammy Sylvia; it's the name of a product you can buy in the grocery store. (Tammy Sylvia's taste buds must have been seared off years ago—can't you tell?) First, she covers the black beans with water and brings them to a boil; then she turns off the heat and lets them sit for 1 hour before she rinses them. Then she puts the smoked neck bones in the Crockpot, adds the beans, and covers 'em with water, adds the onion, bay leaves, red pepper, and Sylvia's Special Seasoning, and turns the Crockpot on high for 2 hours, then to low for 24 hours. The next day, she removes the neck bones, which are then completely naked. She puts the stew in a bowl, covers it with a layer of **Doritos, nacho cheese,** and **the Original Louisiana Hot Sauce,** and she eats it for days on end until it's gone. Tammy Sylvia said each and every time she's been sick—and she's been plenty sick, plenty of times—she's known she was getting well when she craved this dish. We think it may be a substitute for chemo—this or sucking on a flamethrower (oh, sorry, same difference). She may be tiny, but tame, she ain't.

Of course, he's not a Queen, but we love him just as much— Lance Romance, Official Consort to the Sweet Potato Queens, is, in real life, Wilson Wong, hunky husband to the lovely, lucky Lyn and a corporate human resources trainer (Jackson-Wong and Associates—jacksonwong.com). As you know, Wilson is a tall, striking, exotic-looking man with jet-black hair that falls past the middle of his back. If he was a woman, he'd be like Loretta

Lynn—way too old to wear hair that long or that black—but of course, as a *guy*, he looks more fabulous every year. So Wilson goes into a convenience store, no doubt to buy cigarettes, and the clerk, a sweet young thing clearly taken with his appearance, attempts to strike up a conversation by asking him, "So, what tribe are you in?" Dealing with people as he does professionally, he likes to think he's ready for anything, but this one gives him pause, as in, What the fuck is she talking about, what *tribe* am I in? And then he gets it: "Oh, no, I'm *Chinese*," he tells her, smiling. She looks puzzled for a moment and says—she actually says to him—"But I thought Chinese hair was *short!*" Wilson is on the floor, howling. Gathering himself, he manages to tell her, "Well, you're right, it *is* short—if you *cut* it!" and he skipped out the door, laughing all the way. That's the great thing about a culturally diverse group like the Sweet Potato Queens: We just learn something new about other ethnic groups every day. Lord, I swear, people just *will* surprise you, won't they? And every time you think the absolute limit of stupid has been reached, you're so wrong.

Lance Romance and the Luscious Pig

Anyway, when we're lucky, Wilson will make this pig stuff for us—you know how we love food stuff involving pigs. You get a **pork tenderloin** and have the butcher slice it in many, many very thin slices, and you take those home and put them in a Ziploc bag with ½ **cup soy sauce,** ½ **cup sugar,** and a **couple of garlic cloves,** minced. Let them soak in that marinade overnight or even for a couple days. Then you take 'em out and put 'em on a cookie sheet or broiling pan and run 'em under the broiler for a few minutes; flip 'em over, stick 'em back in there for a few more minutes, and then eat 'em all as fast as you can—which you will find is pretty dang fast. You can also do this with plain ole pork chops with happy results—it *is* hard to mess up pig, isn't it?

If you need advice on anything food-related, from olive oil to wine cellars, or if you want to know the best restaurants anywhere in the world from Paris to Rome (the ones in France and Italy, not Texas and Georgia) to Greenwood, Mississippi, we have the Queen who can help you. When she's not in her sequins, Tammy is Carol Daily, owner of the Everyday Gourmet and the Everyday Gardener (theeverydaygourmet.com and theeverydaygardener.com). We seek out and take her advice on a regular basis, and we're in good company: The Viking Range Corporation and Blackberry Farm, among others, are also clamoring for her time and wisdom. Tammy Carol's workweek—jetting off here, there, and yonder—sounds like something in an article out of *Cosmo*. It's all very glamorous-sounding, but it takes a toll: All that wining and dining can turn to dining and *whining* after weeks on end of travel.

Southern mothers are often heard to say about their babies, "She didn't get her nap out," meaning the baby needs more sleep for life to be worth living for everyone. Eventually Tammy Carol has to get her nap out, and her favorite place to do that is on the east porch of her mama's big ole house on the Gulf in Pass Christian, Mississippi. There's a chaise lounge there that calls to

Tammy Carol from any point on the globe and she is drawn to it irresistibly. It is her point of ultimate peace and security. She will go and go and go, and when she just can't go no mo', and you think she will just fall down and sleep on the spot, somehow she manages to get in her car and drive for three more hours to get to that porch. With the centuries-old oak trees making sweet shade and the ceiling fan softly whirring overhead, Tammy Carol can finally *stop*. And when she does, she's just like that baby—whirling dervish one second and out cold the next. Tammy Carol gets her nap out.

Yam Yomp

With a group as large (and hungry) as ours, Tammy Carol is accustomed to making stuff in large quantities; we call it cooking in vats, and it's our favorite thing—wretched excess. If something's good, we want there to be more than plenty of it. We think we're not alone in this. Tammy Carol came up with this vatful of stuff that uses some of our very favoritest things in all the world: sweet potatoes and sweetened condensed milk. My own personal Mother, the ubiquitous MawMaw, came in as I was writing this and insisted that I report on a recent study she read about (and she is standing here looking over my shoulder to make certain that I do). According to her research, martinis, chocolate cake, and cigarettes are False Friends to Women when it comes to comfort; all we really need is—you guessed it—*sweet potatoes!* The article actually says that Sweet Potatoes are a Woman's Best Friend. Well, they're certainly less trouble than a dog, and you *can* eat them, so I'm willing to consider them pals. The piece went on to say that some study done somewhere famous (MawMaw isn't interested in the fine print) showed that women could cut their risk of stroke by as much as 40 percent just by eating a sweet tater every day.

Anyway, for MawMaw and everyone else, here is Tammy Carol's Yam Yomp: Mix up **3 cups quick oats, 3 cups flour, 4½ cups dark brown sugar, 2 teaspoons cinnamon, ½ teaspoon salt, and 1½ pounds butter.** Grease two 9-by-13-inch pans and put a quarter of the mixture in each pan, mooshing into the sides and bottom of the pans, and bake it at 350 for about 10 minutes. While that's baking, get your mixer and beat **4 eggs,** then add **4 cups mashed cooked sweet potatoes,** and **2 14-ounce cans Eagle Brand sweetened condensed milk.** Pour all that into the baked shells and then put the rest of the oatmeal mixture on the top and bake the whole thing at 350 for about 50 minutes. Let it cool a little bit and serve it still warm with ice cream—you might want to put some caramel sauce over the top, just to make sure you get your fat quota in for the day. And don't forget how healthy them sweet taters are for you, so eat up: It's almost like medicine!

As discussed in *The Sweet Potato Queens' Book of Love,* the SPQs are sorta split in the hair department, and it's to the extreme: Some of us have absolutely *the* most fabulous hair on the heads of any humans anywhere and some of us have approximately twenty-eight hairs amongst us, by generous estimates. But of all the crowning glories in our ranks, by far the most glorious belongs to Tammy, or Annelle Primos Barnett to her mommer'n'em. Tammy Annelle's hair is the stuff dreams are made of—if you are one of the hair-impaired, and I am; it's thick and black and vibrant, and I swear it breathes and has independent thoughts. I love to imagine myself with this hair—I can tell you, I would be unbearable if I had this hair. It is purely God's Judgment on me that I do *not* have this hair—same reason I don't have big tits and great legs and a cute ass, because I would no doubt misuse them all. Tammy Annelle's hair is not red, mind you, which is my true dream hair, but when I see it on her head, all thoughts of red leave my mind. I wish I had sultry *black* hair when I look at Tammy Annelle. I can tell you, Tammy Annelle's hair is one of the main reasons we wear wigs with our outfits; if we did not, *she* would be the Boss Queen—or she would certainly dare to try. It's some powerful juju, I'm telling you. Me putting a wig over Tammy Annelle's hair is the same as Delilah cutting off Samson's. Tammy Annelle is a fairly famous interior designer (Annelle Primos and Associates), and people from all over the world who want something made gorgeous track her down and wag her off to their houses to work her magic (and to look at her hair, no doubt). She travels everywhere in the world all the time, either buying stuff for current or future clients or fooling with their houses, but Jackson, Mississippi, is home for Tammy Annelle and her two beautiful baby boys, Arden and Gus. Jackson, Mississippi, is well represented in the person of Tammy Annelle, and also the *voice* of Tammy Annelle. She has, by far, the most decidedly So-o-o-outhern voice of any of us, and so it was with high hilarity that she related this tidbit to us when she returned home from her last trip to New York.

She'd been out shopping all day and the little Yankee girl who helped her at her last stop was totally mesmerized and intrigued by Tammy Annelle's pronounced accent. "Oo-o-oh, I just love to hear you talk," the little girl peeped in her little pursed-up Yankee way, which is impossible for me to describe phonetically, but we all know what it sounds like.

"Where are you from?" she asked.

Tammy Annelle smiled that gorgeous smile and said, "Why-y-y, tha-ank yew, hu-u-u-unny. Whey-ah dew yew *think* ah-m fru-u—uhm?"

"France?" I swear to God was her reply. *France!* Well, there's just not anything I can add to *that*. I'm sure your reaction is similar.

Now, Tammy Annelle is from *the* premier restaurant family in Jackson, Mississippi. For many years, the Primoses have been the proud purveyors of all things garlic to the lucky hungry in town. I bet there is not a single person in the entire metropolitan area who has not eaten in a Primos restaurant at least once. Somebody said something like "If you're looking for good food, find a short Greek." I couldn't remember who said it, so I called the fount of all information, Michael Rubenstein. Rube couldn't remember, either, but he said, "Well, just attribute it to Malcolm. It sounds like something he would say—he probably *wishes* he'd said it and he could use a good quote." So as far as we're concerned, Malcolm White said it, and it is, in any event, true. In Jackson alone, the Greek restaurant dynasty all started with the now-gone-but-still-revered Rotisserie, which was soon followed by the Mayflower and Dennery's and the Elite downtown, Crechale's at one end of town, Marcell's at the other, Bill's Burger House right down the street (now *there's* a misnomer— he ain't makin' no burgers in there), and Primos on the way to the airport. They all have food worth driving and waiting in line for, and they're all run by short Greeks.

Chocolatopolous

Tammy Annelle being one of them, you're probably thinking you will get a fabulous spinach and feta and phyllo recipe called something-something-opolous-opita-ziki or even the world-famous Primos Do-nut Pudding. Well, you're not. Tammy Annelle has two little boys and if you got little boys, you gotta be able to make a kick-ass chocolate cake they can eat right out of the oven with ice cream, so the whole thing will make a big mess on their faces, hands, and all white things in the vicinity.

So here's Tammy Annelle's Chocolatopolous. Mix together in a big bowl **2 cups sugar,** ¼ **teaspoon salt,** and **2 cups flour.** Melt together ½ **cup butter,** ½ **cup vegetable shortening, 3 tablespoons Hershey's Cocoa** (in the brown box), and **1 cup Coca-Cola,** and pour it into the sugar and flour. Stir it all up and add ½ **cup buttermilk, 1 teaspoon baking soda, 2 eggs, 1 running-over teaspoon vanilla,** and a **couple of handfuls of miniature marshmallows.** Pour the mixture into a greased 9-by-13-inch pan. The marshmallows will rise to the top, so make sure they are evenly distributed and there are no glaring marshmallow-free areas in the batter; if you need a few more to fill in the gaps, feel free to add them, but make sure you kinda stir 'em into the batter so they're not just sitting there, naked, on top. Bake this wonderment at 350 for about 45 minutes. But pay attention, you don't want to scorch your marshmallows. (That is just a truism that applies to so many areas of life, isn't it?) At any rate, you want to ice this cake when it's hot, right out of the oven, which is one of my favorite things about it, on account of *that's* when I want to *eat* it, too. So, for the icing, which will also be hot when you put it on the cake (how convenient is that?), take **1 stick butter, 6 tablespoons Coca-Cola, ¼ teaspoon salt,** and **3 tablespoons Hershey's cocoa** (in the brown box), and heat it until it's melted together. Then, over very low heat, stir in **1 box powdered sugar** very quickly (you really don't want to cook this stuff, just melt it), add **1 running-over teaspoon vanilla,** and pour it on the hot cake. Get out your vanilla ice cream, call your baby boys, and have at it! Bibs would be good for everybody.

One more Queen to tell you about. In real life, outside of Queendom, she is Donna Kennedy Sones and she *is* the design firm Hamilton-Kennedy, lock, stock, and many bolts of cloth. Tammy Donna designs and manufactures a positively scrumptious line of women's clothes—all silk and/or cashmere—and she sells them to all the best stores in the country—and also at hamiltonkennedy.com, of course.

Tammy Donna also runs the sweetpotatoqueens.com Web site. Well, that is a big lie. The person who runs the Web site *really* is Alycia Jones, affectionately known as Shipping Tammy, but Tammy Donna answers all the e-mails that aren't directly addressed to me and conducts all manner of other important Web-site *bid'ness*. Tammy Donna and I conduct our Web-site business meetings while we are walking at the Y in the morning. That's when we conjure up SPQ products and such. Unfortunately, we forget 99 percent of it before we get in our cars to leave. I even went so far as to buy a little mini-cassette recorder to tape our conversations, but of course, I haven't remembered to bring it along yet.

A number of mysteries surround these morning walks—like where do all our great ideas go when they fly out of our minds, and how come we can walk and walk and walk until we ought to be just the skinniest things in the world, but, quite to the contrary, we are getting fatter each and every day?! Tammy Donna expressed utter mystification over how it was that *she* was gaining weight when *she* "just wasn't eating at *all*." (I couldn't fail to notice the implication-by-omission that it was apparently *no* mystery at all as to why the excess pounds were finding *me*.) "Well," I said, as kindly as possible, all things considered, "I don't know when it *is* that you think you are *not* eating, because every single time I have seen you or talked to you on the phone for the last month"—both of which are dozens of times every single day—"you were eating or had just *finished* eating or were just *about* to eat—and sometimes all three!" She giggled guiltily, busted big time. So we fell into laughing over ourselves and how we need to fuel the popularity of things like fat arms and gelatinous thighs. I want her to put her clothes-designing talents to work on a whole line of muumuus for us. Muumuus and tent dresses—those were the days, huh? Of course, when they were fashionable, we all weighed about eighty-five pounds and could not even marginally appreciate their airy spaciousness. I keep telling her she could make her fortune creating gorgeous giant dresses that wouldn't touch our bodies anywhere but the neck—doesn't it sound like heaven? Please e-mail her and add your pleas to mine.

Queso~Pig~Etarian Dip

Tammy Donna likes to say that she's a vegetarian. I'm not sure why. She does like salads and lady peas a whole lot and whatever other fresh veggies her sweet mama is cooking today. I do know she won't eat fried chicken unless her mama cooks it—and then really only the pully-bone (wishbone in Yankee-speak); that's pretty vegetarian of her, I suppose. And she definitely won't eat meat in a restaurant except when they put a little meat on the nachos at our Mexican restaurant, and once in a very great while, like on New Year's Eve or at a movie, she'll eat a big sack of Krystal hamburgers—but hardly *ever*, really—and she does get extra onions on hers. And, she does like the ribs from the Exxon station on Northside Drive in Jackson and also their smoked chickens. And sometimes her mama makes those little sausage-ball things that she likes so much. Oh, and bacon, she *loves* bacon. And cheese. Cheese is actually the mainstay of her entire existence. Come what may, Tammy Donna can deal with anything life dishes out, as long as there's some cheese sauce on it.

She has dedicated her life to cheese and performs rededication rituals on a regular basis and she has never met a cheese she didn't love, intimately. So, pretty much, she's a vegetarian—except for bacon and cheese and occasionally, but hardly ever, not even so's you'd notice, a few other delicacies that didn't actually grow in dirt. Well, that's her story and she's sticking to it. I guess you could say she's what, a *queso-pig-etarian?*

Here's her favorite topping for one of her other favorite foods, Fritos Scoops, so beloved because she can pick up so much cheese with them. Mix together **2 cans Mexican corn, drained, 2 cans chopped green chiles, 1 can chopped black olives, 1 cup Hellmann's mayonnaise,** and **8 ounces grated Pepper Jack cheese.** Microwave it all until it bubbles nicely, and top with a **bunch of crumbled-up crispy bacon,** and eat as much of it on your Fritos Scoops as you personally want before serving it to Tammy Donna. She will finish it, I promise.

FINANCIAL TIP

If you can get and keep a bunch of fabulous women friends like these for your whole life, you can save a fortune in doctor's and therapist's bills. Your whole life you've heard that "laughter is the best medicine," right? Well, turns out they were right. So from now on, I'm deducting all Queenly affairs as "medical expenses."

Postscript:
Eatin' and Readin'

The Sweet Potato Queens' Book Club

It's official: We have formed the Worldwide Sweet Potato Queens' Eatin' and Readin' Book Club. All members of the Worldwide Sweet Potato Queens chapters are hereby declared charter members. I am, of course, the Boss of it. In my dedication to this awesome responsibility and my unequivocal devotion to our members, I've compiled our Official Rules and Regulations.

Official Rules and Regulations

1. As the Boss of it, I hereby decree that we will not be reading anything that doesn't perk us up, make us laugh, and/or tell us how to spin straw into gold.

2. We will be reading books that illuminate the power and position of women in society through the ages. Believing that laughter is one of the greatest blessings we're given and we need to take full advantage of it as often as possible, we will look for humor in these books as well.

3. We will not be reading anything about racism, incest, child abuse, war, pestilence, or man's boundless inhumanity to man, woman, child, and beast—and politics is naturally included in nearly all those categories.

4. All reading that is not conducive to a general lightness-of-being or that does not inspire us to realize our true power as women must be done and discussed in secret (with those other book clubs that make you read dark, depressing stuff). I would prefer that our members who do so lie to me about it, if I ask. I like to believe you're doing everything I say.

5. Meetings will be held whenever you damn well please.

6. You can't have a meeting on an empty stomach—everybody will be too distracted by hunger to think about books. Groceries should fall into the accepted SPQ Four Food Groups: sweet, salty, fried, or au gratin. Recommended libations are Fat Mamas' Knock You Naked Margaritas and Revirginators.

7. Feel free to discuss the food and libations consumed during discussion sessions.

8. Try also to discuss the books.

9. Meetings will have a party atmosphere. Wear comfy clothes or sparkly clothes. We all know they don't occur simultane-

ously, so suit your own mood of the moment, but *always wear your crown* and *never wear panties.*

10. Anybody who thinks we're shallow for this can kiss my ass. If they will read some of the posts on our sweetpotato queens.com message board, they will discover the gut-wrenching stuff that some of our members are dealing with in their own personal real lives.
11. See below.*
12. See below.**

Initial SPQ Book Club Selections

Our first official selection for the book club was *A Southern Belle Primer* by Maryln Schwartz. I chose this book because it is purely funny; there is not a dark moment in it. It's a funny Southern book and we are funny Southern women. Since we're a worldwide group, I thought it would be helpful to the spirit of the movement to start with Southern humor—to explain our funny, Southern selves to the rest of the world and also to show that we laugh the loudest at ourselves.

I believe that the ability to laugh at oneself is fundamental to the resiliency of the human spirit. We'll start the ball rolling by laughing first at ourselves, with the strong implication that we will soon move on to laughing at others—all this in the over-riding global belief that the world is now too small a place for there to be an "us" and a "them." It must all be *us,* and we want to do our part to facilitate that.

In the "power and position of women" category, the first books recommended were written by a woman who is the James Duncan Phillips Professor of Early American History and Director of the Charles Warren Center for Studies in American History at Harvard University. The books are *Good Wives* and *A Midwife's Tale: The Life of Martha Ballard Based on Her Diary, 1785–1812*. Their author is Laurel Thatcher Ulrich, Ph.D., and this brilliant, amazing woman is also the originator of an often repeated statement of truth, one that's been reprinted on countless mugs and T-shirts and bumper stickers. Yes, it was our Dr. Ulrich who first said, "Well-behaved women rarely make history."

Official Rules and Regulations, Continued

*11. And so, I want you to close every SPQ Book Club meeting by raising your glasses to toast yourselves, the Worldwide Sweet Potato Queen Movement, and Laura Thatcher Ulrich, saying in unison, with utmost feeling and utter belief in your heart, "Well-behaved women rarely make history." Consider this our motto, our supreme guiding principle, our credo, if you will.

**12. Then go out into the world and demonstrate this credo in the manner most befitting your Queenliness.

APPENDIX

The Queens' Classics

Favorite Recipes from The Sweet Potato Queens' Book of Love and God Save the Sweet Potato Queens

Hardly a week goes by that I don't hear from someone who has *loaned* her personal copy of one of the Sweet Potato Queen books to a friend and now urgently needs a recipe, most often Chocolate Stuff. Let me tell you how we feel about this: It makes us wild! What do you mean you loaned your book to somebody? Have you looked at our photographs lately? We are old women and getting older all the time, and that means there is *right much* plastic surgery that is needing to take place *real* soon, and if you are out there loaning books, we will never get it all done in time to look good in the Box, let alone put it to any good use while we're still ambulatory. We hope everybody's reading the books and doing everything we say and all that, but what we are most vitally interested in is that people are *buying* these books before they read them. These are not expensive books. If your friends are too cheap to buy their own, you need new friends. If you are too cheap to buy them for your friends, they need a new friend.

If you write that your house burned to the ground and your precious SPQ books were lost in the inferno and that you're now in a homeless shelter and want to make Chocolate Stuff for all the people who've been so kind to you—and *if* we can verify your story—we'll gladly send you the recipe. If, however, you have materially contributed to the delay of our plastic surgery by loaning your books to someone, do not expect a favorable response. We think you deserve to be banished to the hinterlands and left without Chocolate Stuff for all time.

Thankfully, we also hear from those of you who are are still in possession of your SPQ books but want to make Chocolate Stuff and just can't remember which book the recipe is in, and you want us to tell you the page number, too. Congratulations! You have achieved just about the perfect degree of hopeless slackassitude for a Queen. We, however, have far exceeded your wildest imagination regarding Lazy, so, naturally, you are out of luck.

Nonetheless, I was overcome with my love and devotion to *you* and *your need* for Chocolate Stuff and all the other sweets, salties, frieds, and au gratins in the other SPQ books. And so, even though it meant more work for me, here they are, all together in one place for your total eating convenience.

Chocolate Stuff

Beat **2 eggs** with a **cup of sugar** and a **half-cup of flour.** Add a **teaspoon of salt.** In the microwave, melt together **1 stick of real butter** (I never use unsalted; I think it tastes flat) and **2 fairly heaping tablespoons of Hershey's cocoa.** Just get regular ole Hershey's in the brown box—anything else is different and will screw it up. Dump the butter-cocoa mixture into the other stuff and stir it up good. Then add **1 running-over teaspoon of vanilla.** I use the real stuff, but the grocery-store kind will not ruin it. Stir that up. Decide on nuts/no nuts. If you go for them, use about **1 cup of chopped pecans.** Pour the stuff into a greased loaf pan and set the loaf pan in a pan of water and stick the whole deal in the oven at about 300 degrees. Depending on how your oven cooks, it needs to stay in there for about 40 to 50 minutes. You can reach in there and sort of tap on the top of it at 40 minutes. If it seems crunchy, I'd go on and take it out. You can't really undercook it, since it's good raw, but you don't want to overcook it and lose the gooey bottom part, which is a crucial factor in the whole texture experience.

Armadillo Dip

You brown a **pound or so of ground chuck** and then pour off the grease. This is purely a consideration for the consistency of the dip and should in no way be construed as a fat-saving measure. Dump in a **bunch of taco seasoning, hot picante sauce,** and hot **Cheez Whiz.** It's sort of like a fancy Ro-Tel dip, only hotter and more fattening, on account of the beef. This stuff is great on Fritos and/or Tostitos, as long as they are not the low-fat baked variety. We are against those. This combo is so hot and so salty that you will quickly need lots of New Allison's margaritas.

New Allison's Mambo Margaritas

These sound weird, if not awful, but I promise, it will be your favorite margarita recipe in the history of the world. You pour in **1 big can of Limeade** (what is that, twelve ounces?), then **1 bottle of Corona beer, 12 ounces of Seven-Up** (never Sprite), and **12 ounces of really good tequila.** Do not attempt to mix this in a blender. You would think that would be so obvious, wouldn't you, what with the beer and the Seven-Up? But we have all done it. Blown the top of the blender and sprayed this sticky mess all over our respective kitchens. Trying to make 'em frozen, don't you know.

Absolut Fredo (a.k.a. Revirginator)

Jeff Good, proprietor of Bravo! (our favorite restaurant), gave us this recipe: **3 parts** (ounces, cups, gallons—whatever) **Absolut Kurant, 1 part Triple Sec,** and **1 part Rose's lime juice.** All this is shaken over ice and served exquisitely in a chilled martini glass.

Coconut Caramel Pie

It really should be called "Oh, God!" First you make one of those crusts, you know, with **1½ cups of flour, 1 stick of butter,** and **1 cup of finely chopped pecans.** You mash all that into a couple of pie plates and bake for 10 minutes or so, at around 350 degrees, just until it gets tan. Then, in a pretty big bowl, mix together—this is so fattening, I can't even say it with a straight face—**8 ounces of cream cheese, a can of Eagle Brand sweetened condensed milk,** and **16 ounces of Cool Whip,** my three favorite ingredients. You put that into the tan pie crusts. Then put **7 ounces of coconut, ½ stick of butter,** and **1 cup of pecans** on a cookie sheet and toast it. You have to really watch it and stir it a lot or the coconut will burn slap up. Put the toasted coconut stuff on top of the pies. Then get a **12-ounce jar of caramel sauce** and pour it all over the tops of the pies. There is absolutely no way on earth to cram any more fat into a single food item. This is it. Freeze 'em for a little while before you try to cut them or you can just sit down in the middle of the floor with a pie and a spoon and have at it. That is my preferred mode of serving.

Hal and Mal's Come Back Sauce

You'll need the following ingredients: **3 cloves of garlic, 2 cups mayonnaise, ½ cup ketchup, 1 cup salad oil, 2 tablespoons black pepper, the juice of 2 lemons, 2 teaspoons yellow mustard, 2 teaspoons Worcestershire, 2 dashes Tabasco,** and **half an onion,** grated. Dump it all in a food processor and whirl away.

Mimi's Butterfinger Cookies

You need **1 cup sugar, 1¹/₃ cups dark brown sugar, 1 stick of butter, 4 eggs** (Mimi used just the whites, but when you read the rest of the ingredients, this seems laughable, like ordering everything on the menu but putting Equal in your tea—to save calories), and **3 running-over teaspoons vanilla.** Mix all that up. Then dump in **2¹/₂ cups chunky peanut butter** and stir that all up. Then you need **2 cups flour, 1 teaspoon baking soda,** and **¹/₂ teaspoon salt.** Get that all worked in to the mix. Now it's Butterfinger time. You can either use the BBs, which is really easy, or you can get just regular ole **Butterfingers—20 or so ounces'** worth—and cut them up and dump 'em in. If you can manage to restrain yourself from eating the entire bowl of cookie dough—which is life-threatening on account of the eggs, but so good, you'd almost be willing to die for it—bake them on a lightly greased cookie sheet at 350 degrees for 7 to 9 minutes, depending on your oven.

Miss Lexie's Pineapple Casserole

You want to drain a **20-ounce can of pineapple** (in its own juice) **chunks or tidbits.** Save **3 tablespoons of the juice** and mix it up with **¹/₂ cup sugar** and **3 tablespoons flour.** Stir that mixture in with the pineapple and **1 cup sharp grated cheese.** I have never tried making this with fat-free cheese and would personally consider the act to be blasphemous, but I have used some reduced-fat cheese when it was all I had and it came out okay. Dump all that into a greased casserole dish. Melt **1 stick butter** and stir it up with **½ cup Ritz cracker crumbs** and put all that on top of the pineapple stuff and bake it at 350 degrees for 20 to 30 minutes, and prepare to be comforted.

Death Chicken

Start off right by lining a 9-by-13-inch pan with **6 or more slices of uncooked bacon.** (We recommend more, naturally. You know, some people like to say "Less is more," but we are just the kind of girls who believe that more is more—and also better.) This is just the perfect start to a perfect ending of just about anything, in my opinion. Next, pour **1 cup uncooked rice** over the bacon. I love it when you don't have to cook the rice first, don't you? On top of the rice, put **some chicken pieces**—happily, the skin must be left on for cooking purposes—and you may use white, dark, whatever you want. **Salt and pepper** the chicken a little bit and sprinkle **a little paprika** over it. Then whisk together **1 can cream of chicken soup** and **1 cup water,** adding **a little bit of garlic salt, a pinch of nutmeg, 1 teaspoon oregano,** and **2 to 3 tablespoons dried parsley flakes.** Pour all that over the chicken and cover the whole deal with heavy foil (emphasis on heavy; it matters). Cook it at 300 degrees for 2 hours, with no peeking.

Connie's Death Corn Five

You take **1 package of yellow rice**—being Southern, we naturally prefer it be Zatarain's. You cook the rice just like the box says, only you don't put any oil in it. Now dump it in your casserole dish (a quart size is probably big enough). Then dump in **1 can Mexican corn, 1 can cream of chicken soup, 1 stick melted butter,** and **1 cup shredded cheese**—cheddar or Pepper Jack, if you like a little kick, which I do. Dump and stir, as I said, and maybe put a little more cheese on top—you can just never have too much cheese, you know—and cook it for about 20 minutes or so at 350 degrees. You *could* make this recipe with nonfat soup, nonfat or low-fat cheese, and Benecol (instead of butter), and it would be pretty low fat.

Larrupin' Good Sweet Potatoes

Okay, to make this larrupin' sweet-potato stuff, you first want to boil a **bunch of sweet potatoes.** You want to end up with about 3 cups' worth of mashed ones, so how ever many taters that is, use that many. You boil the sweet potatoes with the skins on, and after they're boiled, the skins just slip right off in your hand, practically. On the other hand, trying to peel one raw sweet potato, let alone a whole potful of them, would be enough to sour you on this recipe from the get-go.

So boil 'em, then peel 'em and dump them in a big bowl and put in *at least* **1 cup sugar,** ¹/₃ **cup milk, 1 stick butter,** and **1 running-over teaspoon vanilla.** You also need just a **dash of salt** in there or it will taste flat. The sugar part you have to do to taste: Start with a cup, and if it needs more, then by all means, put more. After you get done tasting and testing, then beat in **2 eggs.** Trust me, you do not want to put the eggs in first and then go to tasting it to see if you've got enough sugar in there: The sweet potatoes are just hot enough to make the eggs poisonous but not hot enough to cook them. After all that's done, put the tater stuff in a greased casserole dish. (You can make a vat of this and freeze it.)

The topping is the kicker. You want **1 cup dark brown sugar** (why do they even make the light brown kind?), **¹/₃ cup butter, ¹/₃ cup flour,** and **1 cup pecan pieces.** Stir it all up together and spread it over the top of the taters. My friend Kay North wrote me that she also puts **1 cup of coconut** in this same topping. I tried it and it's a killer. Sometimes I'll make it with coconut on one side and regular topping on the other: This is the height of luxury, I believe. After you put the topping on there, you bake it at 350 degrees for about a half hour.

Country Club Eggs

You start with regular ole **deviled eggs**—you know, mayonnaise, mustard, pickles, paprika, etc.—and you put them in a casserole dish. Put them in there and then as quick as you can (before you eat them all), cover them with **tomato soup** (it could take more than 1 can, unless, of course, you've eaten all but, say, one of the deviled eggs, in which case it won't take much soup at all), and then you cover that with **lots and lots of sliced Velveeta cheese.** Velveeta is just like other cheese in that you can never have too much of it. You bake this concoction at 300 to 350 degrees until it gets bubbly around the edges.

Dinksy's Gooey Bars

You start with a **Duncan Hines devil's food cake mix**—already off to a good start, I say—and mix it up with **1 stick of butter** (not margarine, but I don't think we have to say that, do you?) and **1 egg**. Put it in a 9-by-13-inch pan. Then mix up **8 ounces softened cream cheese, 1 box powdered sugar, 2 eggs, 1 running-over teaspoon vanilla,** and **1 cup chopped pecans** (not walnuts, not almonds—*pecans*). Pour all that over the cake stuff in the pan and bake it at 350 degrees for around 40 minutes.

Bacon Monkey Bread

First you cook a **big wad of bacon.** You're gonna need at least a dozen slices for the recipe, I'd say. Crumble them up (they need to be crumbled for the recipe, but this will also inhibit further pilfering on your part). Mix the bacon bits with **¹/₂ cup Parmesan cheese** and **1 small chopped onion.** Okay, now melt a **stick of butter.** Take **3 10-ounce cans of whomp biscuits** and cut each biscuit into quarters. Dip the biscuit hunks in the butter. Put about a third of them in a lightly greased bundt pan and sprinkle some of the bacon stuff over them. Fill up the pan with layers of buttered biscuit hunks and bacon stuff, ending with biscuit hunks. Bake it at 350 degrees for around 40 minutes, but for goodness' sake, don't burn it. Let it sit in the pan for a few minutes after it's done, and then dump it out onto a platter and jump back to avoid being trampled.

𝒯*winkie* 𝒫*ie*

You start with **Hostess Twinkies**—don't even mention the fat-free variety to me: They are an abomination and should be out-lawed. Cut them in two, lengthwise, and put them in a 9-by-13-inch pan—or whatever size you want, depending on how hungry you are. Then make up some **vanilla pudding**—the kind in the box, whatever brand you grab first, it doesn't matter. Spread the vanilla pudding over the Twinkies. Cover all that with sliced bananas, strawberries, peaches—**whatever kind of fruit you want.** Now, if you are really and truly just absolute total white trash at heart, you may use **fruit cocktail.** Put it in the refrigerator, and when it's cold, eat it until you either get full or sick.

ACKNOWLEDGMENTS

As we have so often said, it is not easy, painless, or inexpensive to be a Sweet Potato Queen. Countless individuals help us every day in countless ways, but *some* of you are doing *more* than others and we would like to recognize you, to thank you, and to encourage you to do even *more* for us in the future, thereby setting a good example for others.

All my True Loves at Crown/Three Rivers: Chip Gibson (even though he's run off to another imprint, I still love him), Steve Ross and Teresa Nicholas (who, along with Sue Carswell, now at *Good Morning America*, are really responsible for my getting published to begin with, so if you see any one of 'em, give 'em a big ole kiss smack on the mouth), Philip Patrick, Brian Belfiglio, Rachel Kahan, Alex Lencicki, Lindsey Mergens, Jennifer Grace, David Tran, Lauren Dong, and Camille Smith. Also:

Steve Wallace and his crew of Random House reps—Toni Hetzel, Laura Baratto, Cole Becker, Eileen Becker, John Hastie, and Bridget Piekarz—for keeping the Queens in the bookstores;

ACKNOWLEDGMENTS

Jenny Bent, who is definitely the cutest and best agent ever, and everybody else at Harvey Klinger who has to fool with me on too regular a basis;

Suzi Altman, for making us look as cute as we really are (see www.suzialtman.com);

Billy, Gabe, Joel, and John at Georgia Carpet Outlets in Jackson, Mississippi, sponsors every year of the Sweet Potato Queens' Ball;

Charly and Bingo and Ann and all the others at Hal and Mal's who go out of their way to make the Sweet Potato Queens' Ball such a Royal Event, and Hal White, who has refrained from murdering any of us and has also mastered the art of Smoked Tuna Dip just for us—thank you very much;

Richard Puckett for letting us use his farm for our float-building fiasco every year;

Brewer Pearson for managing to actually get the float to the parade every year and for doing an excellent Elmer Fudd impersonation;

Brunie Emmanuel, Charles Jackson, and Joe Speetjens—devoted Spud Studs/workhorses;

Everybody at the Cirlot Agency in Jackson, Mississippi—who, along with Jay Sones, make our Web site so fabulous (if you've got something you want to promote, hire these people—trust me);

JoAnne Prichard Morris, the best editor in the history of the entire world, living or dead, for making my pile of papers into a book one more time;

ACKNOWLEDGMENTS

Bad Dog Management, Inc. (bdminc@hotmail.com), for saving my ass a million times;

All the True Queens—all over the world—who have joined our Movement and become a part of the world's only truly inclusive sorority: Pie Kappa Yamma.

ABOUT THE AUTHOR

JILL CONNER BROWNE is the author of the best-selling *Sweet Potato Queens' Book of Love* and *God Save the Sweet Potato Queens*. She is Boss Queen of the now-infamous Sweet Potato Queens of Jackson, Mississippi, and now tours and speaks full-time about all things Queenly.